# THOSE ELEGANT DECORUMS

# THOSE ELEGANT DECORUMS

THE CONCEPT OF PROPRIETY IN

JANE AUSTEN'S NOVELS

JANE NARDIN

State University of New York Press Albany 1973

First published in 1973 by

State University of New York Press
99 Washington Avenue, Albany, New York 12210

© 1973 State University of New York
All rights reserved. Printed in the U.S.A.

Library of Congress Cataloging in Publication Data

Nardin, Jane, 1944–
    Those elegant decorums.

    Includes bibliographical references.
    1. Austen, Jane, 1775–1817—Religion and ethics.
I. Title
PR4038.R4N3        823'.7        73-4821
ISBN 0-87395-236-7
ISBN 0-87395-337-5 (microfiche)

For Terry

# CONTENTS

Acknowledgments      xi

1. How to Read Jane Austen      1

2. The Concept of Propriety      12

3. Propriety as Duty to Society and Self:
   *SENSE AND SENSIBILITY*      24

4. Propriety as a Test of Character:
   *PRIDE AND PREJUDICE*      47

5. Propriety and the Education of Catherine Morland:
   *NORTHANGER ABBEY*      62

6. Status, Work, and Propriety in *MANSFIELD PARK*      82

7. Egotism and Propriety in *EMMA*      109

8. Propriety and the Exceptional Individual: *PERSUASION*      129

Notes      155

# ACKNOWLEDGEMENTS

I would like to thank those who have helped in the preparation of this book. Robert Mayo's seminar on Jane Austen first introduced me to the idea that critical examination of Jane Austen's novels is a way of enjoying them. Joseph Fradin, Robert Hass, Judith Slater, John H. Hagan, Jr., Bernard F. Huppé, and Margaret A. Mirabelli all gave me the benefit of their intelligent advice. I also want to thank Judy Daniel for her help in the preparation of the manuscript. My greatest debt is expressed in the dedication.

# ❦1❦

# HOW

# TO READ

# JANE AUSTEN

In Jane Austen's novels, a person's social behavior is the external manifestation of his moral character. In some of the novels good character is identified rather closely with conformity to the rules of social propriety. In others, it is fidelity to the precepts of a more fundamental "true propriety"—the latter itself variously identified—that provides the standard of virtue. What is common to all the novels is the importance of the concept of propriety in the exploration of the relationship between character and action. At the same time, the role of propriety in the novels cannot be understood apart from an appreciation of Jane Austen's ideas about morality and the techniques she uses to dramatize them.

Several modern critics of Jane Austen's work, though with widely varying degrees of emphasis, hold that irony (or comedy, or satire, as it is variously termed) and morality are basically irreconcilable elements in both her art and her world view. Jane Austen's world view is often termed ironic because it is characterized by a constant awareness of the irresolvable discrepancy between social pretense and moral actuality; and this group of critics, of whom D. W. Harding and Marvin Mudrick are by far the most extreme examples,[1] see her ironic vision of discrepancies between ideals and realities as a destructive implement by which she exposes the corrupt mores of her society. These critics view the moral ideals which Jane Austen presents in her work as "an apostasy from irony,"[2] an uncritical affirmation of the very social mores which her irony exposes as virtually worthless. As a result these critics consider her novels to exhibit a sort of uneasy fence-straddling, in which devastating ironic exposés of the poverty and hypocrisy of conventional morals alternate with dourly conventional endorsements of those morals. They see her novels as flawed works written by a great ironic artist who was susceptible enough to social pressure to betray her genius in the interests of social acceptability and whose talents could not always conceal the fundamental incoherence of her point of view.[3]

Jane Austen was herself aware of the double vision in her art, of the fact as an ironist she would often ridicule aspects of institutions or values, to which as a moralist she gave her basic approval. But she did not find these two modes of viewing the world difficult to reconcile. In her unfinished last novel, *Sanditon,* Jane Austen describes the wellborn, but poor, Miss Denham, who is often rude to her inferiors, flattering her rich, morally repulsive aunt, and comments that the spectacle is "very amusing—or very melancholy, just as Satire or Morality might prevail—Miss Denham's character was pretty well decided with Charlotte" (the sensible heroine of the fragment) (*MW,* p. 396).[4] What Jane Austen means by the term "satire" is merely the humorous awareness of incongruity that modern critics of her work usually call "irony." Ironic doubt and moral affirmation are primarily different moods for Jane Austen, but the conclusions to which either mood leads the thinking individual ought to be similar, if not identical.

Jane Austen can feel this way about irony and morality because her irony is not totally destructive and because her morality is never wholly conventional or uncritical. Irony and morality are far from being irreconcilable elements in her work, for in fact her ironic sense of the irresolvable incongruity between pretense and actuality, the way things are and the way they ought to be, is always employed in the service of morality as she conceived it. Typically she examines moral platitudes in the light of her own sharp ironic perceptions of reality; she rejects what she must, but affirms what she can. For Jane Austen is basically an affirmative novelist. Positive values—good sense, kindness, candor, restraint of egotistical impulses, etc.— abound in her works. Jane Austen affirms much, but she herself is always the independent judge of what to affirm and what to reject in conventional morality. She accepts nothing at all on faith or because social pressure compels her. Irony is characteristically the yardstick by which she measures the adequacy of moral positions in her work and though she considers various values superior to others, Jane Austen never affirms any value as a totally adequate solution for any problem facing the moral individual. Morality for Jane Austen does not consist of swallowing whole the values which society offers her, and her moral affirmations are always qualified by important critical or ironic reservations. When she affirms some of what society offers her, it is not as a completely adequate system of values, but rather as the best available alternative. Unlike many of her critics, Jane Austen views her ironic impulse as the best equipment an intelligent woman living in society can possess, for it enables her to evaluate her society's values and redefine them in a more acceptable and durable form.

A typical example of Jane Austen's moral affirmation occurs in *Pride and Prejudice*.[5] The first half of the novel carefully follows the development of Elizabeth Bennet's prejudiced view of Mr. Darcy's character. Then Elizabeth receives clear proof that she has been wrong about Darcy and realizes that "offended by the neglect" of Mr. Darcy "on the very beginning of our acquaintance, I have courted prepossession and ignorance and driven reason away, where [he is] concerned" (p. 208). She concludes that she has been "blind, partial, prejudiced, absurd" (p. 208). At this crucial moment in the novel, the reader is given a spirited affirmation of how generous candor is superior to quick judgment based on personal whim. Candor is defined by Jane Austen as a willingness to suspend judgment in the absence of wholly satisfactory empirical evidence and to eliminate malice and personal bias, as far as possible, from the process of evaluating others. The quality is exemplified by Jane Bennet, whom Elizabeth, at this point in the novel, admires more completely than she has ever done before. But if we conclude that her conversion to candor is going to solve Elizabeth's problems of judgment we will be missing half the picture. Later in the novel, when Elizabeth realizes that she wants to marry Darcy, but is uncertain whether he still wants to marry her, she decides to use candor in judging his intentions. " 'Let me first see how he behaves,' " she thinks, when he calls at her home, " 'it will then be early enough for expectation' " (p. 355). She watches his behavior carefully, determined not to jump to emotionally biased conclusions, and his attitude continues to mystify her—in fact, she can form no conclusions at all. Candor prevents her from coming to a mistaken conclusion in this case (so it is superior to prejudice), but it does not enable her to judge Darcy accurately, and she finally forms a "desperate resolution" (p. 365) to make him reveal his intentions unequivocally. This is the essential Jane Austen type of affirmation; prejudice is bad, candor is good, but judgment in a complex world will always be mostly a matter of groping in the dark.

The ironies remain here an integral part of the moral prescription: you must be candid in your judgments, but you must also accept the fact that candor will often supply little more than an admission of ignorance. Ironic reservations and moral prescriptions join in Jane Austen's work in qualified affirmations like these. Jane Austen makes us feel that the system of values she endorses is a possible one precisely because she is so clearly aware of its limitations and the novelist who can affirm anything without losing the assent of intelligent readers is a rare thing. Her critical and unsentimental affirmations are capable of convincing at least some intelligent readers that an orderly, dignified, and rational—if not a perfect—life within society, where most of us must remain, is possible. And this unusual achievement is, in part, a result of the alliance between irony and morality in her work.

Conflicts only partially resolved and moral affirmations qualified by ironic reserve are the hallmarks of Jane Austen's world view, no less characteristic of the solemn *Mansfield Park* than they are of the "light, bright, and sparkling" *Pride and Prejudice* (*Letters,* Vol. II, p. 299). To see irony and morality, or criticism and affirmation, as irreconcilable elements in Jane Austen's work is simply to misread her. However, there are aspects of form and technique in her novels which are, in part, responsible for the fact that many critics have seen them as fundamentally inconsistent. Of these, the complexity of narrative viewpoint in the novels is particularly important. Andrew Wright has pointed out that the narrator of Jane Austen's novels "is by turns omniscient and ignorant, humble and sententious, direct and oblique, the dramatist and the teller of tales. Unshackled by more modern theories, her point of view varies: it is sly, often intentionally misleading . . . quite unobtrusive transitions carry the reader from one viewpoint to another and only the closest attention will enable him to ferret out the real intention of the passage in question." [6] This is certainly true—indeed, it does not quite go far enough. Yet a surprisingly large number of critics, deceived by the fact that the narrators of Jane Austen's novels often speak in the authoritative tones of an omniscient narrator in the Fielding tradition, have drawn the erroneous conclusion that all narrative remarks should be accepted at face value as embodying the author's real opinions and intentions. [7] Jane Austen's novels, however, are generally concerned with deception and the reevaluation of more or less mistaken standards of value and in order to make her readers participate in the processes of discovery experienced by her characters, she weaves a narrative fabric of evasions, half-truths, and downright lies, through which the reader must pick his own way. Often not even the closest attention will, as Wright maintains, suffice to ferret out the exact degree of credence Jane Austen the author wishes her readers to give particular narrative statements until the reader has finished the novel and evaluated the statements in question in the light of the book as a whole.

The best way to illustrate and substantiate this claim is to discuss Jane Austen's narrative technique as a series of levels of irony. In speaking of Jane Austen's work, critics generally use the term ironic in two major senses. First, irony may be merely an element of style, a rhetorical device by which the speaker in question says something less, or something more, or something different from what he actually means, leaving his audience to deduce his actual meaning from the immediate context. Thus, for example, when the narrator of *Pride and Prejudice* tells us that Kitty and Lydia Bennet generally walked to Meryton "three or four times a week to pay their duty to their aunt and to a milliners' shop just over the way" (p. 28), readers will realize immediately that no sense of duty is involved in the girls' visits to the milliner and that the use of this inappropriate term is intended to indicate that no real duty is involved in their calls upon their aunt either. Let us refer to this type of irony as "rhetorical irony." In cases of rhetorical irony the passage in question usually carries a definite and unambiguous meaning to the careful reader. But, as we have already seen, the term irony can also be applied to Jane Austen's world view in the sense that she sees an irresolvable disparity between ideal and actuality, between social pretense and moral reality, between the way people are and the way they ought to be, and because she has a sense that all problems are complex and all solutions only choices among evils. The fact that Jane Austen deals only in qualified affirmation is just one indication that her world view is ironic in this sense. Let us refer to this second type of irony as "irony of viewpoint."

Rhetorical irony and irony of viewpoint are very different things and they need not necessarily accompany each other. In Jane Austen's novels, however, they not only accompany each other, but in addition, rhetorical irony merges by subtle degrees into irony of viewpoint—a merging made possible by the author's complex management of narrative point of view. The basic sort of rhetorical irony is, as we have seen, easily identified and understood from its immediate context. However, Jane Austen also deals in ironies which, like simple rhetorical irony, are basically ironies of language, rather than of viewpoint, but which the reader, because he is being made to share in the deceptions of the characters, cannot appreciate until he has read further into the novel. Thus, when the narrator of *Pride and Prejudice* tells us, in an authoritative manner, that Elizabeth owed her greatest relief from Mr. Collins's offensive attentions at the Netherfield Ball to "her friend Miss Lucas, who often joined them and good-naturedly engaged Mr. Collins's conversation to herself" (p. 102), there is nothing in the tone to indicate irony or to tell us—as is in fact the case—that the real point of view here is Elizabeth's mistaken one, rather than Jane Austen's own correct one. It is not until three chapters later that we learn that the adjective "good-natured" was meant ironically here, and that Charlotte's good-nature "had extended farther than Elizabeth had any conception of—its object was nothing less than to secure her from any return of Mr. Collins's addresses by engaging them towards herself" (p. 121).

Jane Austen can produce this sort of irony—let us call it a delayed rhetorical irony because, though it is not clear from the immediate context, when we are later given the relevant information with which to decode it, its meaning becomes unambiguous—precisely because the point of view in her novels is so fluid. She thinks nothing of shifting the point of view at the end of each of several successive sentences, or even in midsentence, and this shift in point of view is only sometimes accompanied by a shift in tone or language that will indicate to the reader what is occurring. Here is an example: the narrator of *Pride and Prejudice* tells us that Mr. Collins, in describing the views from his garden at Hunsford "could number the fields in every direction and could tell how many trees there were in the most distant clump. But of all the views which his garden or which the country or kingdom could boast, none were to be compared with the prospect of Rosings. . . . It was a handsome, modern building well situated on rising ground" (p. 156). In the first sentence here the "trustworthy narrator" is obviously speaking, giving us an acid, external view of Mr. Collins which we can accept more or less at face value and hinting obliquely at the emptiness of Mr. Collins's life and mind. In the second sentence, the exaggerations and pomposity of tone indicate that the point of view is now Mr. Collins's and that the narrator does not by any means endorse his perceptions. The point of view of the third sentence is uncertain. It is probably the narrator describing Rosings in factual language, but it might be Mr. Collins continuing his own description in more realistic terms than before. The narrator may or may not agree that the building is truly "handsome" and "well-situated" (we later learn that Elizabeth finds Pemberley strikingly superior to Rosings). There seems no way of deciding for sure and Jane Austen's novels abound in similar passages, passages in which the source of the point of view or the degree of credence to be given it either can never be precisely determined or can be precisely determined only after the lapse of a number of pages.

The fact that Jane Austen shifts her narrative point of view so freely and that she has absolutely no compunction in stating a falsehood with an air of great authority (as when she remarks that Wickham's conversation was "perfectly correct and unassuming") (p. 72) make complex types or levels of irony possible. In the case of delayed rhetorical irony the reader ultimately learns that he has been mistaken about the point of view or sincerity of a particular passage which he accepted at face value when he first read it. He may discover his mistake in the next sentence, or after three chapters, or not until a second reading of the novel. When he does discover his mistake, however, he will be fairly sure of the precise meaning of the passage in question. So a careful reader of Jane Austen should develop a habit of preserving mental reservations about even the most authoritatively phrased narrative remarks until he is in a position to evaluate them in the light of the entire book. And when he develops this habit of reading with suspended judgment, the manner in which simple rhetorical ironies merge by degrees into ironies of viewpoint or meaning in her work will become clear. Each statement in a novel must be read in the light of all the other relevant statements in that novel. Many ironies (like the one about Charlotte's good nature) of a delayed, but essentially unambiguous, type will appear. For when *Pride and Prejudice* ends, we do know exactly what to think of Charlotte's motives in this episode. But many other ironies which can never be resolved into one valid and simple view, and which therefore are in their essence ironies of viewpoint, will also be revealed by this method of reading. Thus, when we balance Elizabeth's (and the narrator's) energetic rejection of prejudice in favor of candor against her inability to judge Darcey's intentions by the method of candor at the end of the novel, an irresolvable, though clearly stated, irony of viewpoint emerges. And if we continue to apply this method we will find that Jane Austen's works—usually so lucid in their statement of moral and psychological issues—yield some ironies of viewpoint of a still vaguer, more complicated, and less definable sort.

Let us examine, as an example of the most complex level of irony Jane Austen achieves through her devious management of point of view, the statement of the narrator of *Pride and Prejudice* that:

> If gratitude and esteem are good foundations of affection, Elizabeth's change of sentiment [toward Darcy] will be neither improbable nor faulty. But . . . if the regard springing from such sources is unreasonable or unnatural in comparison of what is so often described as arising on a first interview with its object, and even before two words have been exchanged, nothing can be said in her defense, except that she had given somewhat of a trial to the latter method in her partiality for Wickham and that its ill-success might perhaps authorize her to seek the other, less-interesting mode of attachment. Be that as it may . . . (p. 279).

Critics like Laurence Lerner,[8] deceived by the Fieldingesque tone of narrative authority here, disregard the warning of caution given by the last phrase of the passage quoted and use the passage as a whole as definitive evidence for the view that *Pride and Prejudice* is a book denouncing passion and exalting reasonable self-control in matters of love. Yet there is a good deal of evidence in *Pride and Prejudice* which ought to make the reader unwilling to accept the narrator's analysis of the issues in this passage. Elizabeth's excessive reaction when Darcy slights her beauty and the strong feeling in their early verbal sparring definitely indicate sexual attraction between them. Further, in their first long talk, Elizabeth and Wickham, so far from being passionately drawn together, are able to relate to each other only in terms of their mutual interest in Darcy—"after many pauses and many trials of other subjects, Elizabth could not help reverting once more to the first" (p. 82), that is, Darcey's character and behavior. Elizabeth's repeated use of the adjectives "soft" (p. 180) and "gentle" (p. 233) to describe Wickham indicates that, sexually, she does not take him seriously. Darcy, on the other hand, is characteristically "firm" (p. 93). If we remember all this we will be forced to conclude that the situation is far from being the simple opposition of passion and esteem described by the narrator, for it is a psychological tangle of great and ironic complexity. We can never be quite sure, but we may well be left with the suspicion that it was Elizabeth's sexual response to the overpowering Mr. Darcy that, in part, led her to counterfeit to herself a passion for the more easily handled Wickham. The ironic complexities are so subtle here that they defy precise definition.

Simple, resolvable, rhetorical ironies blend by degrees into delayed rhetorical ironies, which merge into clearly defined, but basically irresolvable ironies of viewpoint, and these, in their turn, merge into ironies of viewpoint so subtle and complex that Jane Austen is content merely to hint at them and attempts neither to resolve them, nor to define them precisely. These, roughly, are the levels of irony which characterize Jane Austen's work. And what all this teaches us is that we must never trust the narrator in Jane Austen's novels, no matter how Johnsonian her moral commentaries may sound, for the Jane Austen narrator is merely a complex of functions, rather than a reliable or even consistently portrayed persona. One of the main functions of the narrator in Jane Austen's novels is to present one side, rather than the whole, of the ironic picture when the more complex ironies of viewpoint are at issue. And another function of the Jane Austen narrator is to direct our attention to relevant bits of evidence. She does not, however, generally wish to evaluate these bits of evidence for us—surely all Jane Austen's novels are lessons in learning to think for ourselves—and her narrative comments are not to be accepted as the last word, but are to be seen as only one among many perspectives that may be taken on the action; perspectives that may well turn out to be true, but may just as well turn out partially or completely false. Jane Austen fragments her narrative point of view precisely because the central consciousness behind her novels is one which sees reality as multifaceted.

I do not wish to imply that Jane Austen's novels contain no narrative remarks which are difficult to understand or approve. Jane Austen's brother Henry has written that his sister was rapid and assured in the composition of her novels, but that she revised her manuscripts repeatedly.[9] *Pride and Prejudice, Northanger Abbey,* and *Sense and Sensibility,* at any rate, may be seen as the gradual productions of fifteen to twenty years work. Robert Liddell remarks that "in the palimpsests that her novels are, a word or phrase of pure burlesque will remain [from a juvenile version] either because she let it slip through or (probably more often) because she could not bring herself to sacrifice it to plausibility."[10] This judgment is, I think, correct. I would only add that it appears that Jane Austen was also unable on several occasions to sacrifice a thematically inappropriate epigram or felicitous turn of phrase and that this may be responsible for some of the difficulties various narrative remarks (for example, the famously inappropriate "Let other pens dwell on guilt and misery" of *Mansfield Park* [p. 461]) have caused her critics. However, this probably bothered her very little since her view of her narrators was so highly plastic that she seems almost to have given them the same carte blanche Mr. Elton obligingly bestows on Mr. Woodhouse, in *Emma:* " 'You, Sir, may say anything' " (p. 48)—anything, that is, that seems like fun and doesn't seriously interfere with the business at hand.

By assuming that a certain sort of clever or authoritatively stated narrative comment represents Jane Austen's "true intentions" as to the moral meanings she wished her novels to embody, critics have, in large measure, created the evidences of a simple, dogmatically endorsed moral code, incompatible with her complex ironic vision, that they see in her novels. The narrative praises of Elinor's coolheadedness in *Sense and Sensibility,* or the enthusiastic approval sometimes given by the narrator to "my Fanny" in *Mansfield Park,* need not be seen as somehow inconsistent with Marianne's superior attractiveness or Fanny's repellent censoriousness, as these are embodied in the actions of the two novels,[11] if we realize that we are intended to examine and qualify all narrative statements in the light of what happens in the novels themselves, rather than to accept them as the last word on Jane Austen's intentions of moral meanings. If we read Jane Austen's novels according to this method we will, I feel, do away with many problems of unity that tend to trouble critics.

Jane Austen both understands and controls, through her use of irony, the moral meanings which she wishes her novels to embody. Her novels are made up of "components" interrelated in a complex manner that enables them to comment ironically on each other. And a "component" may be anything from a single word (like the word "good-natured" used to describe Charlotte Lucas in the incident discussed above) to a whole characterization (as Jane Bennet's rather colorless and unimpressive character ironically belittles the value of the quality of candor which she possesses and Elizabeth lacks). Therefore, when something seems puzzling in a particular novel, and especially if it occurs in one of the narrator's remarks, my method of dealing with it is to try to harmonize it with the rest of that novel, before considering the possibility that Jane Austen did not, in fact, know what she was doing, or that the content of her novel was escaping from her control. My assumption is that what is often called inconsistency is really intentional irony or complexity of meaning. Of course, the critic may be justified in concluding that he understands what Jane Austen is doing better than she herself does, that he sees contradictions and inconsistencies of which she was unaware or which she simply didn't or couldn't remedy. But this is often a very risky line to take. The pride of the critic who believes that he sees things which escaped Jane Austen's notice is likely to be punished. And the agency of punishment is simply more careful reading of the novels themselves.

# THE CONCEPT
# OF PROPRIETY

Jane Austen employs a group of loosely interrelated terms to refer
to various aspects of what we would today call "social convention";
that is, to the set of unwritten, but generally agreed upon rules defining socially acceptable behavior in ordinary social situations.
"Elegance," "civility," "propriety," "decorum," and "manners" are
the key words Jane Austen employs to refer to different aspects of
social convention. A closely associated group of terms which refer,
not to social conventions themselves, but rather to the moral considerations which give them their authority are "feeling," "principle," "common sense," and "duty." Together, these two groups of
words comprise the concepts with which this study deals. How does
Jane Austen define them?

Elegance, as it is employed both in Jane Austen's novels and in
the usage of her day, refers to the more superficial aspects of social
convention. To be elegant is to be conventional with style, to follow
the rules of social convention with aesthetic flair and perfect assurance. The important thing to note about Jane Austen's use of this
term is that it has no moral overtones whatever. One can be very
elegant in one's behavior, yet possess little or no moral sense. Lady
Middleton in *Sense and Sensibility,* the Bertram girls in *Mansfield
Park,* and Elizabeth Elliot in *Persuasion* are just a few of the
elegant moral nonentities, concerned with social convention only
as form, who appear in Jane Austen's novels. Lady Middleton, for
example, "piqued herself upon the elegance of . . . all her domestic
arrangements; and from this kind of vanity was her greatest enjoyment in any of their parties" (*S&S,* p. 32). The narrator is
quick to add that to enjoy the forms of socializing, as Lady Middleton does, more than the company of others, is not a very "real"
(*S&S,* p. 32) sort of satisfaction.

Unlike elegance, however, the terms civility, propriety, decorum,
and manners are all characterized both in Jane Austen's usage

and in the usage of her era, by an important duality of meaning. One meaning of each term refers to social acceptability, the other to moral appropriateness. Let us take propriety—for Jane Austen the most important of these words—as an example. In Jane Austen's time, according to the *Oxford English Dictionary,* propriety could mean "conformity with good manners or polite usage," in other words, what is conventional and socially acceptable; or alternatively, "fitness, appropriateness, suitability . . . and conformity . . . with principle," that is, what is morally valid (*O.E.D.,* Vol. VIII, p. 1484). Thus, when Jane Austen uses the term propriety, she can mean either outward conformity with an external set of social conventions or adherence to morally acceptable patterns of behavior, which may or may not also be socially acceptable.

Jane Austen uses the term decorum as virtually synonymous [1] with the term propriety. In *Northanger Abbey,* for example, after Catherine Morland has been warned by Mr. Allen that she ought not to be taking unchaperoned drives with John Thorpe, she remarks that she would not have gone driving at all had she " 'known it to be improper' " (*NA,* p. 105). After thinking the matter over, she concludes that it would be kind for her to write to Isabella Thorpe—who has been taking the same sort of unchaperoned drives with Catherine's brother, James—to "explain the indecorum of which [Isabella] must be" unaware (*NA,* p. 105). Thus, Catherine describes the same action as both improper and indecorous—and there is nothing in Jane Austen's usage of these terms elsewhere which indicates that Catherine is making a semantic mistake in using them as synonyms.

Jane Austen employs the word civility to refer to conformity with the less important social conventions—conventions governing common, everyday politeness, rather than conventions governing action and decision in the more crucial areas of life. When Charlotte Lucas, for example, is prevented from leaving the Bennets's breakfast room "by the civility of Mr. Collins," we know that the term refers only to certain formal conventions of behavior—in this case, "very minute . . . inquiries after [Charlotte] herself and all her family" (*P&P,* p. 114), whom he hardly knows at all—which Mr. Collins is employing in a meaningless manner. But Jane Austen also refers to civility as one of the "lesser duties of life" (*S&S,* p. 347). When used in this sense, civility means the debt of everyday attention, consideration, and kindness which we owe to our acquaintances, regardless of the particular forms in which it is expressed.

Manners may (like elegance) refer to the externals of social behavior, but the word may also be used to refer generally to the way a man treats his fellows in society. Thus when Elizabeth Bennet says that the manners of Mr. Bingley's two sisters "are not equal to his" (*P&P,* p. 15), she does not mean that Mr. Bingley's manners are more polished or socially correct, but simply that he treats new acquaintances more kindly and considerately than they do.

The term principle, duty, common sense, and feeling, as Jane Austen employs them, are closely associated with the concepts of civility, manners, propriety, and decorum. They are the moral absolutes which stand behind the moral meanings of these dual terms. When, for example, the term propriety is used merely to mean the forms of socially acceptable behavior, it has no particular connection with principle, duty, common sense, or feeling. But when the term is used to mean morally appropriate social behavior, then it also means, for Jane Austen, behavior in accord with principle, or duty, or good sense, or good feeling—or all four. The key terms Jane Austen employs to describe various aspects of her ideas concerning social convention may be seen as forming a spectrum of meaning beginning with the purely social and merging into the purely moral realm of discourse. Elegant behavior is simply socially acceptable behavior. The terms civility, propriety, decorum, and manners, like elegance, refer merely to socially correct behavior, but they can also be used to describe morally valid behavior. Principle, duty, common sense, and feeling, are the purely moral considerations which ought to motivate social behavior. I chose propriety as the central term of this study of the connections between morally valid and socially acceptable behavior because it applies to a wider range of social behavior than does the term civility and because Jane Austen uses it more frequently than she does the virtually synonymous decorum. There is a sense in which manners—for example, in the phrase "the manners of the age" (*NA,* p. 200)—is used, like propriety, to refer to the entire range of social behavior governed by convention. However, the term also has the more restricted meaning of an individual's style in handling social forms. Therefore propriety, which always refers to rule-governed social behavior broadly defined, seems a better choice than manners for this general study of Jane Austen's ideas about social convention.

The duality of meaning which characterizes the terms civility, propriety, decorum, and manners, is important in Jane Austen's thinking about society. The general term propriety may refer to a set of socially acceptable rules of behavior, or it may refer to a morally acceptable code of behavior. For the sake of a convenient terminology, let us refer to the first sort of propriety as "conventional propriety," to the second sort as "true propriety." An important question which Jane Austen asks in each of her novels is: What is the relationship between conventional propriety and true propriety? Do the socially acceptable and commonly accepted rules of social behavior, in other words, provide a reliable guide to a morally acceptable standard of social behavior? What considerations give true propriety its legitimate authority over individuals in society? When we examine in detail the answers Jane Austen suggests for these basic questions in each of her novels, we discover that, while the most important aspects of her ideas remain pretty much the same, the details are characterized by experimentation and variation, rather than by calm certainty. From the beginning to the end of her writing career, Jane Austen maintains her view that propriety is true propriety only if it is backed up by solid moral considerations. An ethic of propriety which consists of following the forms of conventional propriety for no other reason than that they are in general use, is never, in Jane Austen's view, a valid one. True propriety can only spring from some sort of sincere moral commitment to self and others in society. However, though the forms of conventional propriety are never enough in themselves, in practice, when the moral commitment is present, the conventional forms generally prove to be a fairly satisfactory guide to morally valid social behavior. That true propriety must have a moral aspect, but that its external manifestation does not differ very radically from conventional propriety narrowly defined, are constants throughout Jane Austen's writing career.

However, Jane Austen's ideas about propriety do change. In large measure the changes are due to the fact that she is dealing with different thematic problems in each novel and these different problems to some extent dictate different treatments of the propriety theme. Because Jane Austen is attacking the cult of excessive feeling in *Sense and Sensibility,* it becomes almost a necessity for her to emphasize the formal, conventional aspects of propriety at the expense of those aspects which spring from good feeling toward others. Similarly, in *Emma,* it is the characterization of Emma herself which defines how questions about propriety are formulated in that novel. It is Emma's basic quality of defensive egotism which motivates her rule-oriented ethic of propriety and hence controls the way the propriety theme functions in the novel as a whole. Yet even beyond this there remain variations in her handling of the propriety theme which are obviously due to her continued consideration of the concept and its implications.

When we come to analyze the precise nature of the moral commitment which converts conventional propriety to true propriety—that is, the moral considerations which give propriety its legitimate authority over individuals—we find Jane Austen experimenting with a variety of answers. And though her writing indicates that conventional propriety provides a fairly workable guide to morally valid social behavior, just how close the identification between true and conventional propriety turns out to be, changes from one novel to another. In *Sense and Sensibility,* Jane Austen considers the possibility that the external manifestation of true propriety may in fact be *identical* to the conventional rules of propriety. Perhaps, she suggests in this novel, some of the conventional, commonly accepted rules of propriety represent the best ways past society has devised for dealing with the common problems of social life and derive their authority simply from the fact that they work more efficiently than any conceivable substitute. Or perhaps, she suggests, again in *Sense and Sensibility,* some of these common rules of propriety are the terms of a just and workable social contract, defining what each man owes to his fellows in society in return for the benefits he himself receives from the existence of society. In *Pride and Prejudice,* Jane Austen wonders whether true propriety may not be a very slightly modified version of conventional propriety, in which the commonly accepted social conventions are followed when they seem sensible, moral, and functional to the intelligent individual, and are altered (as little as possible) when they do not. In *Pride and Prejudice* a distinction is made between basically moral rules of propriety, which must be obeyed, and rules which are only matters of fashion or convenience, and which may therefore be violated if common sense so dictates. In this novel, therefore, true propriety is conventional propriety purged of its debased elements and justified by a close connection with sound common sense and good common morals. In *Northanger Abbey,* a conception of true propriety very similar to that of *Pride and Prejudice* is developed—but it is worked out in a less formal and abstract manner. In *Mansfield Park,* Jane Austen wonders if true propriety may not, very simply, be the outward, social manifestation of an inward commitment to a set of elevated moral principles. More strongly than in her preceding novels, Jane Austen here suggests that the standard of socially acceptable behavior current in the fashionable world of her era is a corrupt one—corrupt because it has become almost totally divorced from the moral principles which she sees, in *Mansfield Park,* as the only justification for a true standard of propriety. In *Emma,* Jane Austen considers the possibility that true propriety may be the spontaneous, inwardly prompted social behavior of people whose feelings toward their fellow men are generous and good. In *Emma,* the divergence between conventional propriety—essentially a matter of rules—and true propriety—defined and justified here as the spontaneous manifestation of good feeling—though still slight, is somewhat greater than in any of Jane Austen's earlier novels. A truly proper man, in this novel, may act in accordance with a conventional rule of propriety. He does so, however, not because it is a rule, but only because his best feelings prompt him to follow it—and there is a viable possibility that he may choose to disobey it if his feelings so dictate. Good feeling alone justifies this standard of propriety. In *Persuasion,* Jane Austen examines these questions more uneasily than at any other time. The questions are asked and considered in great detail, but the answers suggested are qualified by so many ironic reservations that they can scarcely be called answers at all. What this novel does, essentially, is to examine two contrasting standards of propriety. A propriety of rules justified, as in *Sense and Sensibility,* by their efficiency and their connection with the idea of duty to self and society is here considered in conjunction with a spontaneous and informal propriety justified, as in *Emma,* only by the impulse of intelligent, well-intentioned individuals.

These ideas concerning the moral considerations which give a code of propriety its legitimate authority, though they are clearly distinct from novel to novel, are not radically different, or in most cases mutually incompatible. The good sense and good morals which justify true propriety in *Pride and Prejudice* and *Northanger Abbey* are not hard to harmonize with the moral principle which justifies propriety in *Mansfield Park,* or even, basically, with *Sense and Sensibility*'s concept of duty to others. Most of the variations are variations of emphasis, altered treatments of an idea whose essence remains pretty much unaltered. Similarly, the variations in Jane Austen's ideas concerning how closely the individual ought to feel himself bound by the conventional rules of propriety when these conflict with other moral considerations are, in most of the novels, variations only in degree—for all the novels, except *Sense and Sensibility,* allow some measure of individual discretion on this point.[2]

Are there, then, *any* elements in Jane Austen's ideas about propriety, as these are developed in her novels, which cannot be reconciled with each other? Ultimately, only a few aspects of the propriety theme in *Sense and Sensibility* prove basically incompatible with that theme in the later novels, especially *Emma* and *Persuasion.* In *Sense and Sensibility,* Jane Austen develops the idea that the moral consideration of duty to self and others dictates strict obedience to the whole conventional code of propriety, no matter what other considerations of feeling or judgment urge the individual to set that code aside. In *Emma,* however, it is the feelings of moral individual, not the rules of society, that dictate the minutiae of social behavior. Where in *Sense and Sensibility* the individual's moral sense dictates strict obedience to conventional rules, in *Emma* the same moral sense dictates occasional disobedience. In *Emma, Pride and Prejudice, Mansfield Park,* and *Northanger Abbey,* however, virtually all the rules of propriety under consideration are rules governing everyday social interactions. Examples include the rule prohibiting young ladies from taking long country walks alone (*Pride and Prejudice*), the rule forbidding a person to break a social engagement because he has received a second invitation (*Northanger Abbey*), or the rule that social calls must be returned (*Emma*). For the sake of a consistent terminology, I shall in future refer to these rules of decorum which dictate behavior in everyday, relatively unimportant social situations as the "minor rules" of propriety. In *Emma, Mansfield Park, Northanger Abbey,* and *Pride and Prejudice,* it is the minor rules alone which are under consideration. In *Sense and Sensibility,* on the other hand, Jane Austen considers and endorses both this sort of minor rule and the more serious rules of propriety governing behavior in crucial social situations where there is a good deal at stake. Examples of this second sort of rule are the rule prohibiting young ladies from behaving as if they were engaged to men who have not proposed to them, or the rule that a disappointment in love should be concealed from the world. In future, we will refer to these serious rules of propriety as the "major rules" of propriety. The major rules of propriety are merely assumed to be valid in *Pride and Prejudice, Northanger Abbey, Mansfield Park,* and *Emma*—the value of these rules is neither seriously questioned nor critically examined in these four novels. In her last completed novel, *Persuasion,* Jane

Austen takes cognizance of the fact that her ideas about the strict obedience due to the minor rules of propriety have altered since she wrote *Sense and Sensibility* and she reopens the question of whether the major rules of propriety are still as sacrosanct to her as they were when she considered them in *Sense and Sensibility*. Whether under the stress of the particular artistic problems she was treating, or because her own ideas about propriety had really changed, or, as I think, from a combination of both causes, Jane Austen, in this retrospective novel, *Persuasion*, sets many of her earlier thoughts about propriety in a new artistic context. This time, however, she is unable to solve the problem of what true propriety is and what gives it validity nearly as neatly as she did in the earlier books which treated the subject in a more restricted manner.

These distinctions between major and minor and basically moral and merely fashionable rules of propriety, unlike the words propriety, elegance, civility, manners, and so forth, have no warrant in Jane Austen's own language. The terms are my own inventions. I use them because I believe that in various novels Jane Austen separates out one or more groups of rules for special consideration; in other words, that she often tacitly divides the rules into classes so that she can handle questions of propriety in a more complex and sophisticated manner. My purpose in giving my own names to these classes or groups of rules is simply to provide the reader with a terminology that is at once detailed enough to permit him to see which rules of propriety are at issue in a given novel and consistent enough from novel to novel so that Jane Austen's various ideas about propriety can be compared. However, it must be understood that I am not claiming terribly much for these terms as tools of explanation or comparison. The rule of propriety stating that a visitor must wait to be admitted by a servant and the rule stating that one must not break an engagement merely because one has received a second invitation both fall into the class of minor rules governing everyday social interactions. Yet they have all sorts of differing implications and it is only in terms of what they have in common—that they regulate ordinary social situations in which nothing crucial is at stake—that they can be compared. The reader should keep these qualifications in mind in reading what follows.

A few words concerning the precise nature of the conventional code of propriety by which the gentry of Jane Austen's time regulated their social life will, I think, make it easier for the reader to understand what follows. For the gentry of Regency England there were unwritten, but precise and unmistakable, rules of propriety governing a multitude of social situations. The steps by which an acquaintance, or a dinner party, or a courtship was to proceed were rigidly and minutely prescribed for people of comparable social rank. Twentieth-century American readers, at any rate, are unlikely to have any personal experience of such a detailed, all-encompassing code of propriety. And it is precisely the rigidity and minuteness characterizing this conventional code of propriety that supply Jane Austen with one of her most effective tools as a novelist. Jane Austen believes verisimilitude in recording the subtleties of social behavior to be part of her duty to her audience. At the height of her own writing career, she made some rather detailed criticisms of a novel written by her young niece Anna Austen and these criticisms show her to be intensely concerned with accuracy on minor questions of propriety: [3]

A few verbal corrections were all that I felt tempted to make— the principal of them is a speech of St. Julians to Lady Helena— which you see I have presumed to alter—As Lady H is Cecilia's superior, it would not be correct to talk of *her* being introduced; Cecilia must be the person introduced (*Letters*, Vol. II, p. 387).

I have also scratched out the introduction between Lord P and his brother and Mr. Griffin. A Country Surgeon (don't tell Mr. C. Lyford) would not be introduced to men of their rank. —And when Mr. Portman is first brought in, he wd not be introduced as the Honble.—*That* distinction is never mentioned at such times;—at least I believe not (*Letters*, Vol. II, p. 394).

Let the Portmans go to Ireland, but as you know nothing of the manners there, you had better not go with them. You will be in danger of giving false representations. Stick to Bath and the Foresters. There you will be quite at home (*Letters*, Vol. II, p. 395).

Give her a friend and let that friend be invited to meet her at the Priory, and we shall have no objection to her dining there as she does; but otherwise a woman in her situation would hardly go there before she had been visited by other families (*Letters*, Vol. II, p. 400).

Sir T.H. you always do very well; I have only taken the liberty of expunging one phrase of his, which would not be allowable. 'Bless my Heart!'—It is too familiar and inelegant (*Letters,* Vol. II, p. 400).

Several points can be deduced from this insistence on verisimilitude where propriety is concerned. It seems clear that Jane Austen assumed the novelist's audience—most of whom were older and more experienced socially than Anna herself—to be well acquainted with the conventional code of propriety applicable to the characters in a novel. She believed that therefore the audience would notice even small deviations from the code and would assume that there ought to be a reason for those deviations. Finally, Jane Austen held that since deviations from a precise code of propriety would be spotted by a novel's readers, the novelist should use such deviations only as a means of revealing character and should be careful not to confuse the issue by making random errors.

This last, of course, is Jane Austen's own invariable practice and there is no act of impropriety in her novels from the smallest gaucherie to the most serious piece of malicious rudeness that is not there for the purpose of revealing something about a character by means of that character's failure to abide by a rule of propriety with which she assumes her readers to be familiar. Although this would seem to imply that the modern reader, unversed in the minor points of Regency etiquette, will be at a serious disadvantage in reading Jane Austen's work, in actuality this is not the case. Jane Austen's novels are composed of a multitude of details as precisely interrelated as pieces in a jigsaw puzzle, so that the meaning of any detail can usually be deduced from its relationship to the others. When Mrs. Elton, for example, refers to her husband as "Mr. E," and to Mr. Knightley simply as "Knightley," we do not need to be up on contemporary forms of address to realize that she is being vulgar, for the contrast between her forms and those used by Mrs. Weston or Mr. Knightley will tell us all that we need to know, if we are willing to make a slight effort that Jane Austen's contemporaries did not need to make. From the complex interrelation of detail within each novel we can deduce enough about Regency codes of manners in polite society so that we will not miss nuances that were obvious to Jane Austen's contemporary readers. Indeed, it would be only a slight exaggeration to say that each of Jane Austen's novels is an autonomous world, holding within itself virtually all the information that is needed to understand it. Jane Austen assumed knowledge of a precise conventional code of propriety in her readers, but she relied upon that knowledge only to make it somewhat easier for her readers to comprehend her subtleties—the most important guides to her meaning are never to be found outside her novels.

In each of her novels, then, Jane Austen takes for granted the existence of a precise and detailed conventional code of propriety with which both the novel's readers and the more genteel of the novel's characters are familiar. All deviations from this code have a meaning; all reveal something about character. I earlier explained that the word propriety (like the words civility, manners, and decorum) is an ambiguous one in Jane Austen's usage, for it may refer either to conventionally acceptable social behavior or morally valid social behavior. As one might expect, therefore, deviations from the conventional code of propriety in Jane Austen's novels may have either social or moral significance. When a character's failure to obey a conventional rule of propriety results from ignorance or misapprehension concerning the nature of that rule the deviation is primarily social. When Catherine Morland agrees to take unchaperoned drives with John Thorpe, this disregard of the rules of propriety governing the relations of young ladies and young gentlemen reveals Catherine's ignorance of the usages of polite society. Mrs. Elton's use of excessively informal modes of address reveals the fact that she has lived in the sort of inferior society that mistakes affected ease for aristocratic breeding. These two acts of impropriety type Catherine and Mrs. Elton socially: Catherine is inexperienced, Mrs. Elton is underbred. The moral overtones are secondary. With ease and precision, Jane Austen uses this rigid and detailed code of propriety to locate characters in their proper positions on the social scale.

But a more important function served by the existence of this code of propriety is the revelation of moral and psychological aspects of character. Because in Jane Austen's work the relationship between conventional propriety and true propriety is neither simple, nor unchanging, what a particlular deviation from a rule reveals about a character's moral condition is not always immediately apparent. It is only as Jane Austen develops her ideas concerning the nature of true propriety in a particular novel that the relationship of various characters' behavior to the different rules of conventional propriety assumes its final significance. In *Emma,* for example, it is only after

Jane Austen has fully demonstrated that true propriety means social behavior springing from generous feelings toward others, that the reader fully realizes that Emma's conventionally polite behavior, because it merely glosses over her hostility to others, reveals moral weakness, rather than moral strength. A character's social behavior —in other words, the standard of propriety by which he lives—is, for Jane Austen, the external manifestation of his internal moral and psychological condition.

# PROPRIETY
# AS DUTY TO
# SOCIETY AND SELF:
## *SENSE AND SENSIBILITY*

How can an intelligent individual manage to survive in society at once satisfying its demands upon him and preserving his own integrity of judgment and feeling? This question crops up again in Jane Austen's later novels—most notably in *Mansfield Park* and *Persuasion*—but in none of them do we get quite as vivid or horrifying a picture as *Sense and Sensibility* provides of a voracious social milieu eagerly pressing upon the sensitive and intelligent individual, ready to devour his time, his privacy, his freedom of action, and ultimately his sense of his own uniqueness as a person. For in none of Jane Austen's other novels is the heroine surrounded by such an extensive and almost unrelieved collection of incredibly stupid, insatiably curious, and irresistibly sociable acquaintances as fall to the lot of *Sense and Sensibility*'s dual heroines, Elinor and Marianne Dashwood. Their only sensible or basically likeable acquaintances are their mother, Col. Brandon, Edward Ferrars, Willoughby, and Mrs. Jennings. And Mrs. Jennings, though full of good will and common sense, is so gossipy and curious as to prove a frequent source of torment to both heroines, whose privacy is further invaded by the intensive, if unperceptive, scrutiny of Sir John Middleton and the elder Miss Steele. Sir John and his wife are so unable to be alone that their constant invitations leave Elinor and Marianne little time of their own while at Barton Cottage. When they go to London, the distasteful social demands made upon their hours are, if anything, even greater.

The picture is an unpleasant one, for we see the heroines forced into continual contact with people who are either imbeciles like Charlotte Palmer, Miss Steele, or Lady Middleton, or hopelessly unfeeling, like John and Fanny Dashwood. Social events here are dull at best, but more typically painful. The quintessential social occasion in this novel is the John Dashwoods' dinner party, a party at which "no poverty of any kind, except of conversation, appeared . . . almost all [those present] labored under one or other of these disqualifications for being agreeable—Want of sense, either natural or improved—Want of elegance—Want of spirits—or want of temper" (p. 233). Thus the novel postulates a society at once extremely dull and extremely demanding—and the question of how the heroines are going to defend their time and privacy against its attacks, yet remain, as they must, members of it,[1] is therefore a real and important one.

At the beginning of *Sense and Sensibility,* Marianne and Elinor advocate very different systems of dealing with this society, and the novel as a whole represents a complex testing of the adequacy of their methods. Elinor's system is by no means faultless, but it proves vastly superior to Marianne's. Its several elements can be, and often are, characterized by the term sense (as Marianne's views can be described by the term sensibility). Since these terms are misleadingly simplistic, however, I do not intend to use them here, but instead shall try to break down Elinor and Marianne's complex views on the proper relationship of the individual and society into several elements and discuss the adequacy of each of these elements separately. The title of this novel, which has implied to many readers a one-to-one relationship between the heroines and the qualities of sense and sensibility narrowly defined, has probably been responsible for more critical misunderstanding than anything contained in the body of the work.

Before considering Elinor and Marianne's systems of dealing with society, however, I want to discuss further the distinction between major and minor rules of propriety which runs through the following chapters. What I refer to as the minor rules (the term is mine, though the basic distinction is Jane Austen's) are those governing everyday social interactions where no really serious consequences are likely to result from any particular decision on a question of propriety. The minor rules govern such matters as behavior to hosts and guests at social events, paying formal calls, or forming a new acquaintance. What all the minor rules have in common is that they regulate aspects of social interaction which come up repeatedly and frequently in everyone's life and, for that reason, are not points in which anything permanent is at stake. If a person is rude to his guests on one occasion, he may be able to mend his mistake on the next—and if he cannot repair the breach, he still has probably not done anything that will radically affect his fate in life. The major rules, on the other hand, by definition regulate the really important decision points of social life, points at which there is a great deal at stake. These crucial decision points are the ones which come up only a few times in any individual's life: forming an engagement to marry, or helping one's son choose a profession are examples of this sort of decision point. If the individual behaves wrongly in such situations, his whole life is likely to be seriously affected. One's conduct of the most important social and familial relationships—for example, those of parent, child, husband, wife, lover, fiancé—also falls under the regulation of the major rules of propriety. For an individual's success or lack of success in handling these relationships (like his behavior at key decision points) is likely to have far-reaching effects upon his life, because these are the close ties which both define a person socially and satisfy him emotionally. That is why I classify the rules of propriety defining the conventional way to conduct these relationships as major rules. This distinction between major and minor rules is an approximate one at best, but I think it is clear in most cases and making it will help us analyze Jane Austen's ideas about propriety. And this distinction, as we shall see, is particularly significant in the world of *Sense and Sensibility*.

Elinor's system of dealing with society (as represented by the people she knows) begins with the primary assumption that the individual has a duty to all his acquaintances. The basic source of this duty is never explicitly stated, but it is very clearly implied that all men benefit in numerous ways from the existence of society, and, this being the case, it is only fair that each should be willing to sacrifice something to the smooth functioning of that society. In other words, society is founded on a social contract. The minor rules of propriety which dictate behavior in ordinary everyday social situations seem to Elinor to be a fairly satisfactory guide to what the individual owes his acquaintances in society and this is one reason why she follows these rules scrupulously. When Marianne adopts Elinor's original viewpoint at the end of the novel, she refers to "the civilities, the lesser duties of life" (p. 347), and this phrase articulates the concept of true propriety which is present throughout. Propriety of behavior is part of a duty to society, one of the terms of the social contract, and it consists in giving others their due social observance. This does not, of course, mean that one must be exquisitely polite to everyone at all times. It implies only the duty to be as attentive to others as they deserve—in terms of the ordinary, minor rules of civility—regardless of how unpleasant it may be to the individual to give that attention. Elinor always does what is "necessary in common civility" (p. 170), but she proportions her attentions to the merits of the recipients and is really cordial only to those who, in her opinion, deserve it.

The concept of propriety, however, includes more than mere politeness. Conventional propriety of behavior means giving acquaintances their due, but it also means following various major rules of conduct that, either primarily or solely, affect the well-being of the self. Two major rules which are important in *Sense and Sensibility* are the prohibition on writing letters to a man to whom you are not formally engaged and the injunction that a love affair ought to be concealed as far as possible until it culminates in a proposal. These two rules are primarily intended to protect the individual against some of the serious humiliations and pain that an unrequited attachment can create. The individual's obligation to respect these rules is basically a duty he owes to himself. This sort of major rule of propriety is justified solely by the assumption that it works well for individuals and not by any connection with the idea of duty to others under a social contract. Both Elinor and Marianne form unrequited attachments and Elinor deals with the situation by following the major rules of propriety: that is, by concealing her love and attempting to repress it. Marianne, on the other hand, tries to make her own rules. Jane Austen uses this situation as a test case for the major rules of propriety.[2] Elinor's conduct of her unhappy love affair attests to her belief that individuals can get along more comfortably in society if they conduct their most significant relationships according to the conventional rules, even where those rules are repugnant to their feelings. We will later examine, in greater detail, Elinor's reasons for holding this belief.

How one regards propriety is thus very important in reaching an accommodation with society. And another major aspect of life in society—upon which one's views of propriety also bear—is the question of judging other individuals in it, for if one is forced to interact with others, one must either be sure of what sort of people they are or run the risk of being hurt. One function the rules of propriety have is to structure social situations and therefore to make judgment easier. If a young man does not propose to a girl, for example, she had better not assume he is planning to marry her: the proposal alone is an unambiguous indication of his intentions (if, like most people, he is playing by the rules).[3] In judging social situations, Elinor generally assumes that the people involved are indeed obeying the rules of propriety and that the clues provided by those rules may therefore be relied upon. Thus, when she sees a letter from Edward to Lucy Steele, Elinor immediately concludes that the two must be engaged. The rules of propriety here provide Elinor with an aid to judgment, but other aids are obviously also necessary. So in general, Elinor also assumes that people have rational motives for their actions and that prosaic explanations of their motives are likelier to be true than romantic ones. These assumptions, like her assumption that people usually obey the rules of propriety, help her to structure complex situations and hence make them easier to evaluate (though not, as we shall see, necessarily easier to evaluate correctly). Elinor's usual method of judgment is inductive. She gathers all the relevant facts at her command, however little likely they are to be of use (thus, she even asks the witless Charlotte Palmer for information concerning Willoughby's character) and, as far as possible, tries to draw unbiased inferences. Where the evidence is obviously ambiguous, she tries to suspend judgment and wait for clarification, in the meantime placing people's motives in the best possible light—the method Jane Austen calls candor. On judgments reached by these means, Elinor bases her relationship to society.

Point for point, Marianne's views on how to deal with society are very different from Elinor's. Where Elinor bases her dealings with her acquaintances on a desire to give everyone his due, however little she feels like giving it, Marianne is governed purely by impulse in her relations with society. Elinor is trying to live up to an ideal of a moral duty to society embodied in the minor rules of propriety, but Marianne believes that her first duty is to herself and consists of an obligation to express her feelings freely.

Marianne fails to realize how much she benefits from the existence of an ordered society. The idea that she owes her dull, disagreeable acquaintances payments of civility in return for boring her at parties never enters her head. Marianne's ideas are, of course, the result of her adherence to the cult of sensibility so important in the popular fiction of the day. It is not necessary here to discuss this cult in detail,[4] we need only note that its basic tenet was the belief that individuals possessing strong, sympathetic feelings would find these feelings a pretty safe guide to moral reality. Refined sensibilities could through their inherent power of sympathy, penetrate easily through the social veneer to the basic worth of people and customs. Accepting these assumptions, Marianne naturally concludes that in following the dictates of her feelings (since obviously *she* is a person of sensibility), she is also living up to the demands of the highest type of morality. Thus, when acquaintances annoy her, Marianne feels justified in expressing her irritation and the "usual inattention to the forms of general civility" (p. 144) that results sometimes rises to downright rudeness under more extreme provocations. Marianne judges others' "motives by the immediate effect of their actions on herself" (p. 202) and when they offend her sensibilities treats them as if they had been guilty of flagrant immorality—the natural result of making personal feeling a moral yardstick.

Marianne's adherence to the cult of sensibility not only causes her to disregard the forms of common politeness but also gives her a rationale for ignoring the major rules of propriety. Marianne believes that her sensibilities give her a moral sense that is a far more infallible guide to truly reasonable and moral social behavior than the commonly accepted rules of propriety can provide. Thus, in her view, the belief that this sort of rule ought to be followed because of its wisdom is totally invalid. When Elinor criticizes her for a serious breach of propriety, Marianne replies that " 'if there had been any real impropriety in what I did, I should have been sensible of it at the time, for we always know when we are acting wrong, and with such a conviction I could have had no pleasure' " (p. 68). So Marianne feels herself perfectly free to disregard all the ordinary rules governing courtship that do not suit her feelings and to behave, on several occasions, as if she and Willoughby were formally engaged, when no proposal has been made.[5] The major rules of decorum suggesting caution and concealment during courtship seem "commonplace and mistaken notions" (p. 53) to Marianne; she has greater faith in her own reason than in the sort of accumulated social wisdom the major rules of propriety embody and she acts on her own conclusions in large matters of propriety as well as small.

Elinor is careful to form her own personal judgments of people and ideas, but she always acts conventionally (thus, though she and Edward love each other, she never even considers encouraging him to break his engagement with Lucy, which he could easily do).[6]

Marianne, however, always acts upon her own judgments in opposition to convention so that the accuracy of her conclusions is of
vital importance to her. In forming her judgments of people and
things, Marianne disregards the clues that the rules of propriety
ought to provide (thus she feels herself "solemnly engaged," [p.
188] to a man who has not proposed). And she is not very interested
in gathering evidence ("'Seven years would be insufficient to make
some people acquainted with each other, and seven days are more
than enough for others,'" she tells Elinor [p. 59]). Instead, Marianne
relies, as usual, on the ability of her refined sensibilities to give her
clear and realistic knowledge of the world around her. Though
Elinor's method of judgment is inductive and Marianne's is intuitive, each sister believes herself to be a true devotee of reason.

Where Elinor relies on the concept of duty, on the conventional
rules of propriety, and on empirical judgments to structure her relationship with society, Marianne relies, almost entirely, upon feeling. We can now examine how well each sister succeeds in structuring her relationship to the society of *Sense and Sensibility;* the
strengths and drawbacks inherent in each system of preserving the
individual's time, sense of himself, health, and self-respect against
the attacks and demands of a voracious and sometimes hostile society. And we shall discover that, though Elinor's system is ultimately justified, it is by no means completely superior, point by
point, to Marianne's. The narrator's remarks about Elinor are almost always made in highly respectful tones, but we ought not to
let this blind us to the fact that there is a great deal more covert
irony at Elinor's expense than most critics have noticed.[7]

The individual's relationship with society must, of course, be
vitally affected by his methods of judging people and ideas. Perhaps,
therefore, it will be wise to begin by examining Elinor and Marianne's contrasted methods of judgment to discover which sister
bases her interaction with society upon a shrewder perception of its
realities. Marvin Mudrick has justly observed that, though Elinor
and Marianne go about making their judgments so differently, their
opinions about their acquaintances are actually quite similar.[8] They
are both well able to estimate the worth of their brother and his
wife, of the Middletons, the Palmers, and the Miss Steeles; they are
both guilty, though Marianne more so, of underestimating Mrs.
Jennings. Initially they even agree in their estimates of Willoughby's
character. And further, when they disagree, it is by no means always
the case that Elinor is right and Marianne wrong. For we will dis-

cover that Jane Austen is making the point that just as judgments based on immediate feeling are likely to distort reality, so careful and candid empirical judgments, like Elinor's, carry within themselves their own peculiar tendencies toward error.

When Col. Brandon mentions to Elinor, with embarrassment, that he once knew a young lady who resembled Marianne, Elinor "connect[s] his emotion with the tender recollection of past regard" (p. 57), but carries her conjectures no farther. The narrator, speaking from Elinor's point of view, then comments that in the same situation, "Marianne . . . would not have done so little. The whole story would have been speedily formed under her active imagination; and everything established in the most melancholy order of disastrous love" (p. 57). This sounds like simple irony directed against Marianne, but we later learn that Col. Brandon's love story was of precisely the lurid sort Marianne would have imagined.[9] In this instance, Elinor, because she has refused to conjecture, has made no actual error, but her rejection of what she thinks Marianne might conjecture points up the first characteristic flaw in her mode of judgment. Elinor, the inductive, has seen that most people's lives are fairly prosaic, conventional, and rational, and she tends to assume that the wild improbabilities of romance never actually occur. But it is Jane Austen's point that occasionally they do occur—perhaps this is the thematic, as opposed to the plot, function of Col. Brandon's inset tale of melodramatic woe—and that when they do occur it is the one with the lively imagination not the one with sound common sense, who is likely to understand them. Kenneth Moler points out that when Marianne falls ill, Elinor persistently underestimates the signficance of her sister's illness just because of her sensible conviction that young women die of broken hearts only in sentimental novels.[10] Marianne is her mother's favorite daughter and this point comes up so frequently in the course of the novel that we may be sure it rankles in Elinor's bosom.[11] Mrs. Dashwood favors Marianne precisely because of the strong sensibility they share and Elinor, less well-endowed in this respect, asserts her claim to be an equally valuable individual in her own right by overemphasizing the importance and worth of the prosaic, unromantic aspects of life which her mother and sister despise. Perhaps Elinor wishes to deny the validity and value of the character traits that are responsible for the tie which binds Mrs. Dashwood so closely to Marianne.

Elinor has, in fact, assumed a good deal more propriety and rationality than actually exist, and these assumptions warp her judgment. Thus, when Elinor sees Marianne writing to Willoughby "the conclusion which as instantly followed was, that . . . they must be engaged" (p. 161), an inference that proved correct in the case of Edward and Lucy's correspondence. But Elinor's conclusion here is false precisely because she has overestimated the binding force of convention on Marianne. Similarly, when Elinor receives the false report of Edward's marriage, she is able to supply a rational explanation of all its details: Lucy has hurried on the marriage through a fear of losing Edward and they are "going down to Mr. Pratt's, near Plymouth" (p. 355), for an economical honeymoon. We can hardly blame Elinor for failing to penetrate the true nature of the case; the interesting point is that the simple, rational, coherent explanation she devises is false, for what has really occurred is wild and irrational. Actually, Lucy has entrapped the pseudosophisticated, ambitious Robert Ferrars and they are travelling to Dawlish apparently because it is the only town in Devonshire of which the groom has ever heard (for earlier it had "seemed rather surprising to him that anybody could live in Devonshire without living near Dawlish," [p. 251]). Thus, Elinor's attempts to deduce conclusions from her assumptions that people are generally rational and conventional are not always totally successful. The forces of emotion and irrationality are sometimes more potent than she is willing to admit.

Candor—making allowances for people's difficulties, placing their behavior in the most charitable light, and suspending judgment in the absence of satisfactory evidence—though in general a good idea, also has its drawbacks as practised by Elinor. When Elinor and Edward first became acquainted, it is evident that he admires her, but his behavior is oddly inconsistent and often cold. Marianne, then and later, notices an "unaccountable coldness . . . a deficiency of all that a lover ought to look and say" (p. 87) on Edward's part. She senses something radically wrong, though she is mistaken in assuming that the cause is probably the fact that Edward and Elinor have weak feelings. But Elinor, so well used to weighing probabilities and making reasonable allowances for the necessary imperfections of life in society, explains away all Edward's oddity on the basis of the fact that he is financially unable to marry, placing "all that was astonishing in his way of acting to his mother's account . . . [she was] very well disposed on the whole to regard his behavior with all the candid allowances and generous qualifications" (p. 101). In fact, Elinor's valuable social habit of making allowances

for the difficulties under which people may be laboring has led her
to commit the serious mistake of falling in love with a man who,
consciously at least, never meant either to court or to deceive her
—a less justifiable mistake than Marianne's with Willoughby, who
did indeed intend to propose. And this is the problem with candor
and generosity of judgment: although it saves you from con-
demning hastily and unfairly, it exposes you to the danger of ex-
plaining away and excusing too much.

It might be objected here that candor does not cause Elinor's
mistake about Edward, but rather that Elinor's wish to believe
herself loved by him warps her judgment. The narrator tells us,
after all, that the sort of candid allowances Elinor spontaneously
makes for Edward "had been rather more painfully extorted from
her, for Willougby's service, by her mother" (p. 101). This is true,
of course, but the point Jane Austen is making through Elinor's behavior in this incident is that the attempt to be unbiased and generous and to base judgment only on evidence can never entirely
succeed, for the bias of feeling is always creeping in. Jane Austen
seems to believe that, though fancy and reason are indeed two
different things, no individual is completely capable of separating
them in judging matters that affect him deeply. Take, for example,
the following narrative passage, written from the point of view of
Fanny Dashwood:

> It so happened that while [Fanny's] two sisters . . . were first
> calling on her in Harley-street, another of her acquaintances had
> dropt in—a circumstance in itself not likely to produce evil to
> her. But while the imaginations of other people will carry them
> away to form wrong judgments of our conduct, and to decide on
> it by slight appearances, one's happiness must in some measure
> be always at the mercy of chance. In the present instance, this
> last-arrived lady had so far allowed her fancy to outrun truth
> and probability, that on merely hearing the name of the Miss
> Dashwoods, and understanding them to be Mr. Dashwood's
> sisters, she immediately concluded them to be staying in Harley-
> street (p. 248).

The irony here is obvious: the visitor's deduction, which Fanny
Dashwood sees as wildly fanciful, is, though mistaken, quite rational. Fanny cannot admit this, because to admit that her visitor
is being rational is to acknowledge that her sisters-in-law ought indeed to be staying with her. And even the restrained, honest Elinor

is not free of this kind of distortion where her feelings are deeply involved, nor is the method of candid judgment, seemingly so empirical in nature, by any means immune to bias.

Marianne, on the other hand, makes no attempt to judge inductively and carefully, nor does she generally assume that her acquaintances are rational, conventional, and unromantic. Empirical evidence, of course, obviously affects her judgments, but it affects them only through the medium of her feelings. Openly displayed cruelty or stupidity, for example, may make Marianne dislike someone, but she acts on her dislike without trying to determine the exact nature or empirical validity of its cause. Since Marianne is sensitive and intelligent, her feelings, as Mudrick notes, often lead her to the same opinions as Elinor's induction, for she registers intuitively the same evidence that Elinor enters into her carefully kept balance sheets.[12] And occasionally the sympathetic imagination which Elinor tries to repress in herself does lead Marianne to leaps of insight of which her sister is incapable. Thus, on the strong empirical evidence of Col. Brandon's well-documented tale of Eliza Williams, Elinor concludes Willoughby to have been a hardened libertine who callously sported with Marianne's affections and possibly even intended to seduce her! His eleventh-hour explanation surprises her and throws her off balance in direct proportion to the strength of her erroneous, though empirically based, conception of him. Marianne, however, is never entirely convinced that Col. Brandon's tale represents the true Willoughby. Against its hard evidence of immorality and the additional evidence provided by his callously worded letter of rejection, Marianne balances her own intuitive sense that Willoughby has loved her passionately, and is willing at least to hope that he was "only fickle, very, very fickle" (p. 345), rather than cruel or immoral. And in fact Marianne's imagination has supplied her with the key to Willoughby's behavior—so it is not surprising that the revelations of his confession do not shake her view of the matter nearly as deeply as they did Elinor's.

In stating the drawbacks of Elinor's methods of judgment and the strengths of Marianne's, I do not mean to imply that, in the last analysis, they are of equal worth. To assume rationality and conventionality, to judge cautiously by evidence, proves correct more often than to assume that life resembles romance and to judge quickly by feeling and intuition. Marianne—Mudrick notwithstanding—does make more mistakes than Elinor: she underestimates

Col. Brandon, overestimates her mother, is slower to discover Mrs. Jennings's real worth, and much slower to notice something odd in Willoughby's behavior. By suspending judgment, Elinor is sometimes able to correct mistaken first impressions, but Marianne judges once and for all. Still, on balance one cannot attribute to any striking superiority of judgment the fact that Elinor survives the disasters of *Sense and Sensibility* so much better than Marianne. The difference in the accuracy of their ideas is not great and the point is clearly made that Elinor's methods have their own serious drawbacks. For the sources of Elinor's success we must, therefore, look to those two aspects of social relationships that are more directly related to the question of propriety—its major laws and minor laws—as a regulator of social action.

"'My doctrine,'" Elinor tells Marianne, "'has never aimed at the subjection of the understanding. All I have ever attempted to influence has been the behavior'" (p. 74). Though Elinor forms her own ideas about people and events, she is deeply convinced that it is her duty to obey the rules of propriety, no matter what strong and reasonable considerations may urge her to set them aside. Here is an example: when Edward refuses to break his engagement to Lucy, his only reason is that he believes her "to be a well-disposed, good-hearted girl, and thoroughly attached to himself" (p. 367), so that to break the engagement with her would be really cruel as well as technically dishonorable. Elinor, on the other hand, is well aware that Lucy is selfish and ambitious and couldn't care less about Edward, yet Elinor "gloried in his integrity" (p. 270) when he re-affirmed his engagement. There is an important difference here: Edward is mostly concerned with what he believes to be Lucy's feelings, but Elinor merely wants him to obey the letter of a law of honor, in spite of the fact that every other reasonable consideration (Edward's love for her, hers for him, Lucy's corruption and indifference) suggests that the rule ought to be set aside in this specific situation. For it is Elinor's basic conviction that the rules of propriety ought to be followed strictly, no matter what sacrifices are involved. And since Elinor always obeys the conventional laws of propriety, her personal judgments are expressed overtly less often than Marianne's—for in Marianne's view, personal judgment, not conventional propriety, should be the ground of action.

The minor laws of propriety, common civility or the rules governing everyday social interaction, are as sacrosanct to Elinor as the most significant, morally oriented major rules of propriety. Elinor is ca-

pable of putting people down, but she always does it politely. She is
as incapable of rudeness or even informality as she would be of
adultery or murder, simply because she believes strict civility to be
part of the duty she owes to her acquaintances, part of her debt to
society. Elinor tries to fulfil this duty, but she doesn't find it an easy
one. *Sense and Sensibility* is full of phrases indicating the unpleasantnesses in which Elinor's conscious politeness involves her. "Upon
Elinor the whole task of telling lies when politeness required it,
always fell" (p. 122), Elinor always takes possession of the "post of
civility" (p. 160), and when confronted with impertinent curiosity
she "obliged herself to answer" (p. 181). She "was obliged to listen
day after day" (p. 214), to the stupid and the dull. She was often
"worried down by officious condolence" (p. 215), and was frequently
"forced to use all her self-command" (pp. 217–218) to stay polite. She
often "wished to talk of something else, but" (p. 239) was rarely
successful in changing the subject. These are just a few random examples of the social martyrdom Elinor's courtesy imposes upon her.
Marianne, on the other hand, is quite willing to be rude to those
who annoy her and generally disposes of them quite effectively.
Elinor confesses to having " 'often wished [her sister] to treat our
acquaintances in general with greater consideration' " (p. 94), but
she has failed entirely. Since Marianne is willing to take summary
measures to rid herself of at least some unwanted social obligations,
she is able to live a semiprivate life in society which is much more
pleasant than Elinor's social existence. At the Middleton home
Marianne plays the pianoforte, while Elinor suffers at the card table
with her hostess. At the Palmers's Marianne displays "the knack of
finding her way to the library, however it might be avoided by the
family in general [and] soon procured herself a book" (p. 304),
while Elinor carries on a most uninteresting conversation with Mrs.
Jennings and Charlotte.[13] At Gray's shop, Marianne is "as well able
to collect her thoughts within herself and be as ignorant of what
was passing around her . . . as in her own bedroom" (p. 221),
while Elinor fumes with irritation at Robert Ferrars's lengthy delib-
eration over a toothpick case.

What Jane Austen wants readers to infer from all this is not that
Elinor is having as painless a time in society as Marianne—she
certainly isn't—but rather that the luxurious power to withdraw
from unpleasant society is purchased for Marianne by the excess of Elinor's social martyrdom. Elinor and Marianne almost
always go about together in society. Acquaintances tend to regard

them, not as individuals, but as a sort of social unit: the Miss Dashwoods. Elinor knows that social observations paid by her alone will
generally be credited by the world to both Miss Dashwoods. When,
for example, Elinor pays a visit of duty to the ailing Fanny Dashwood, she cancels a family obligation for both herself and Marianne.
Further, since the two sisters are almost invariably together in society,
Elinor is often able, by excess of civility or other maneuvers on her
own part, to conceal Marianne's deficiencies. Thus, when Marianne
ignores her hostess, Mrs. Jennings, on their journey to London,
Elinor "to atone for this conduct . . . took immediate possession
of the post of civility . . . behaved with the greatest attention to
Mrs. Jennings, talked with her, laughed with her, and listened to
her" (p. 160), and succeeded in her object of protecting Marianne
from censure. Part of the reason why Marianne gets along as comfortable as she does is that her debts to society—debts which society
never, in Jane Austen's view, allows to go long unpaid—are being
discharged by Elinor. And Jane Austen's rather uncharacteristic use
of a military metaphor ("the post of civility") to describe what
Elinor is doing for Marianne carries with it an implied comparison
of ordinary social life to the front lines in battle. We may wish that
we could live in society the way Marianne does, accepting its benefits as Marianne accepts, for example, the joy she derives from Sir
John's frequent parties during her love affair with Willoughby, but
refusing to sacrifice time or pleasure to its demands. But Jane Austen
is making the point here that society exists as a contractual arrangement. If society gives, it also takes; and if an individual refuses to
make the sacrifices it asks, those sacrifices must be made by someone
else.

Thus there is a strong element of unconscious selfishness in
Marianne's refusal to consider politeness a duty. In caring so much
for her own feelings, she ignores the feelings of others, particularly
those of Elinor. And selfishness is by far the deadliest sin in the
world of *Sense and Sensibility*.[14] In this novel, the worst form of
selfishness is the ambition to rise in the world socially or financially.
Ambition is the farthest extreme of mercenary "sense" and it characterizes all the really bad people in the novel: Lucy, Col. Brandon's
unprincipled father and brother, Mrs. Ferrars, and the John Dashwoods. It also proves to be Willoughby's downfall. The reasonably
estimable characters are marked by a general contentment with
what they possess, financially and socially, provided it enables them
to live fairly comfortably. Ambition, in *Sense and Sensibility*, is seen

only as the desire to rise at the expense of others (and this is why is is an aspect of selfishness), a willingness to sacrifice "time and conscience" (p. 376) for money. The ideal of society postulated here is essentially a static one—a world in which duties (politeness, charity, etc.) and privileges (income, rank, and so on) are equitably balanced so that no one receives more than he repays. Ambition is the desire to upset this static contractual balance in one's own favor, to assume privileges while refusing to discharge duties (as Lucy, for example, is willing to benefit in every possible way from her engagement to Edward, but does not feel her self bound to him by the duties of fidelity and loyalty).[15] Thus, ambition is opposed both to human values and to a sense of duty, and one sign of this opposition is the fact that ambitious people are generally polite only where they think it will pay. John Dashwood, for example, on first meeting Col. Brandon "eyed him with a curiosity which seemed to say that he only wanted to know him to be rich, to be . . . civil to him" (p. 233). Marianne obviously does not display this worst sort of "cold-hearted selfishness" (p. 229), but the impulsive, egotistical, warm-hearted rudeness of her sensibility and the self-serving civility of mercenary sense resemble each other in that both spring from those basically self-regarding motives which equate duty to society with duty to self. True civility consists of obeying the minor rules of propriety and paying what is due, not just which you feel like paying. And this is as true for a loving person like Marianne as it is for the closed-hearted John Dashwood.

Elinor's view of civility as a duty, then, makes her something of a social martyr and through her Jane Austen makes the point that, for the intelligent, life in a society composed mostly of the average must in some important ways be an hourly martyrdom. This martyrdom can be avoided only by imposing it on somebody else. Thus, it is suggested that Marianne's attempt to act upon her personal judgments in her everyday social interactions is basically impossible; society exacts conventional behavior in exchange for its necessary benefits and Marianne has been free only because Elinor has paid her share. Perhaps a part of Elinor's willingness to be martyred in this way may be traced to her desire not to feel inferior to the league of Mrs. Dashwood and Marianne from which she is somewhat excluded—for surely an elder sister who continually pays a younger sister's debts may be legitimately proud of herself. Elinor is certainly pleased when Marianne finally acknowledges the debt she owes her sister: " 'But you,—you above all . . . had been wronged by me . . . Your example was before me, but to what avail?—Was I more considerate of you and your comfort? Did I imitate your forebearance, or lessen your restraints, by taking any part in those offices of general complaisance or particular gratitude which you had hitherto been left to discharge alone?—No;—not less when I knew you to be unhappy, than when I had believed you at ease, did I turn away from every exertion of duty or friendship . . . leaving you . . . to be miserable for my sake' " (p. 346).

And what about Marianne's attempts to act upon her own judgments in those larger matters of propriety that deal with defining conventional ways of handling the most important relationships and situations in social life? These major rules of propriety are commonly supposed to represent the most effective ways society has found for dealing with the significant difficulties of social life, but are they indeed more effective than the solutions which the rational, intelligent individual can devise for himself? To this question, Elinor answers yes; Marianne, who opposes "the subjugation of reason to commonplace . . . notions" (p. 53), no. Marianne's judgment, we have noted, is not much worse than Elinor's, but the fact is that both sisters, though well able to judge obvious cases like John Dashwood or Charlotte Palmer, make innumerable errors of judgment throughout the novel, ranging from the trivial to the vitally important. The basic problem of *Sense and Sensibility* is not the interpretation of personality. Jane Austen assumes here that even the best judges are very fallible interpreters of personality, and the basic problem in the novel is how people can protect themselves from the consequences of misjudgment, rather than how they can best avoid making mistakes (this question comes up, but it is of lesser importance). Everyone in the novel misjudges Willoughby and Edward until after the essential damage has been done to Marianne and Elinor. And to this basic question of how the damage may best be repaired, the major rules of propriety are most relevant. For the major conventions of propriety which govern behavior in really important social situations generally suggest caution, reserve, and suspension of action. If you act on individual judgment at all, these rules imply, you'll probably regret it; better wait. And in a world where judgment is as uncertain as it is in *Sense and Sensibility,* rules suggesting the concealment of feeling and hesitation in action are indeed likely to prove beneficial, simply because reason, feeling and intelligence are not, as Marianne erroneously believes, reliable guides to action.[16]

Elinor never acts on the convictions of her own intelligence in opposition to convention. She conceals her love for Edward because he has not proposed formally, though she is fairly sure he loves her. She acts the part of a woman whose heart is untouched. Elinor's refusal to act on her belief that Edward loves her, as Marianne acts on a similar belief in writing to Willoughby, saves her from the sort of open rejection which Marianne meets. But though the caution that the conventional rules of propriety suggest can indeed spare the individual this type of public humiliation, if the rules cannot spare him some of the suffering that comes with even the best concealed defeat, they aren't really improving matters all that much.

When we examine Elinor's continual stress on concealment and reserve we find, I think, that it is somewhat excessive and unjustified. Elinor thinks that frankness had better be avoided because it will expose "you to some very impertinent remarks" (p. 68), but as Marianne observes, Elinor's own reserve is no guarantee against the Middleton-Jennings brand of impertinence. Elinor's caution conceals little from the one person she really wishes to deceive—Lucy—and conceals so much from everyone else that it ends by depriving her of necessary sympathy. After Edward's engagement becomes public, Elinor finds she has so well deceived her family by playing the role of indifference, that she cannot help wondering sadly "whether her mother ever recollected Edward" (p. 355) or sympathized with her sorrow. Further, hearing Elinor advising Marianne to let her enemies "be cheated of their malignant triumph" (p. 189) by seeing how calmly she bears Willoughby's desertion, we expect a hostile, or at least insensitive, attack on Marianne's grief by society—an assault which, like most of the hostility and criticism Elinor fears, fails to materialize. In fact, everyone behaves quite well, and even Mrs. Jennings and Sir John avoid mentioning the matter in Marianne's presence. The one hostile remark, made by Lucy—" 'Perhaps, Miss Marianne, . . . you think young men never stand upon engagements if they have no mind to keep them' " (p. 243)—Marianne calmly and sublimely ignores.

Because Marianne has almost no feeling of being vitally involved with society, for good or ill, she can disregard a great many social unpleasantnesses as beneath her notice. But Elinor, who is intensely aware of being in a close contractual relationship with society—a relationship which is difficult and time-consuming—takes social unpleasantnesses much more to heart. Because she gives so much to society, Elinor tends to be irritable and defensive about what she considers to be legitimately her own. Elinor's sense of the need for privacy and the potential hostility of the world outruns reality and is in two important senses self-defeating, since it both gives her the morbid sensitivity of a person with a secret to protect and cuts her off from the sympathy she really needs. Elinor had made a fetish of privacy and this is one undesirable result of her taking the conventional rules of propriety so seriously—though some of her stress on concealment and reserve must be seen as a reaction against the spontaneity advocated by her mother and Marianne.

The efficacy of Elinor's sense that it is a duty to handle love relationships in the cautious, reserved way prescribed by conventional propriety is not to be found—as she herself erroneously believes—even partially in the need to protect one's private feelings against contempt and hostility. Rather, Elinor's behavior works out well because the necessity to conduct a love relationship in the way prescribed by the conventional rules of propriety—that is, the necessity to play the lover in accordance with a particular, socially defined role—helps control an individual's destructive emotions. Jane Austen makes the point, in several novels, that one cannot play a social role, like that of the reserved lover, for long without permanently altering one's personality for better or worse. In *Mansfield Park,* she considers the possibility that chronic role-playing may destroy the capacity for sincerity, but in *Sense and Sensibility* her concern is mostly for the good effects of playing the conventional roles prescribed by the major rules of propriety for handling life's most serious relationships. The emphasis here is not, as in *Mansfield Park,* on the possibility that frequent changes of role will destroy the capacity to feel, but rather upon the possibility that feeling uncontrolled by a set of rules prescribing a sensible social role may destroy the entire personality. We are intended to believe, however unconvincingly this is effected, that Elinor's love for Edward is originally of comparable strength to Marianne's for Willoughby—in each case a feeling of great and potentially destructive power. Marianne, exaggerating her emotions and indeed trying to play the role of a sensibility heroine, surrenders herself to the power of feeling; Elinor, playing the uncommitted role the rules of propriety dictate, resists it. And Marianne plays her role so successfully that she comes close to destroying her ability to give it up when she decides to do so. When Willoughby leaves Devonshire, Marianne feeds her grief by every possible means "til her heart was so heavy that no further sorrow could be gained" (p. 83). So when Willoughby finally rejects her, Marianne is already well-versed in her role of heroine and responds to Elinor's plea that she exert herself to repress her sorrow, by crying, "'I cannot, I cannot . . . Oh! how easy for those who have no sorrow of their own to talk of exertion'" (p. 185). Later, when Marianne realizes that this accusation has been unfair and that Elinor has indeed suffered, but with fortitude, she wishes to give up her own role as a sensibility heroine and to behave as Elinor has behaved: "She felt all the force of that comparison [with her sister] . . . with all the pain of continual self-reproach; regretted most bitterly that she had never exerted herself before; but it brought only the torture of penitence without the hope of amendment. Her mind was so much weakened that she still fancied present exertion impossible" (p. 270).

Marianne's unrestrained feelings have gradually produced a sort of mental deterioration and she has actually very nearly become the kind of young woman she originally, but mistakenly, fancied herself: a heroine whose feelings are so strong that she has no power to combat their effects and to whom a disappointment in love must therefore bring a broken heart and a speedy death. For Jane Austen's point here is not that novels of sensibility overestimate the power of the emotions [17]—feeling can indeed kill in *Sense and Sensibility*—but rather that emotion is potentially so powerful, and in some situations so destructive, that the "indulgence of feeling" (p. 83) which is the sensibility novel's stock-in-trade is a dangerous game. Marianne and her mother enjoy exaggerating their grief at the death of Henry Dashwood, and this is safe because the emotion involved, though genuine, is not frighteningly intense. Mrs. Dashwood has her beloved daughters to maintain her interest in life, and Marianne, though she loved her father, has everything before her and is in no danger of deciding to follow her parent to the grave. But to indulge so exclusive and intense an emotion as Marianne's grief at losing Willoughby is virtually suicidal. Just like a real sensibility heroine, Marianne nearly dies. The sombre tones in which the episode of her putrid fever is painted hint that unrestrained feeling is not titillating, but wasteful and tragic. Elinor has earlier teased Marianne about her literary fascination with the "flushed cheek, hollow eye, and quick pulse of a fever" (p. 38), but Marianne's own romantic fever is in no sense amusing. "Hour after hour passed away in sleepless pain and delirium on Marianne's side, and in the most cruel anxiety on Elinor's" (p. 312). If one plays a role that demands indulgence and increase of feeling, one is likely to be destroyed physically, as well as mentally, precisely because the power of feeling is so great.

Elinor, who, we are meant to believe, originally feels a grief as great as Marianne's, chooses to play a very different role, the role of a young woman who can control her feelings in order to spare herself and those around her from their destructive power—a role prescribed, not by the cult of sensibility, but by the rules of propriety. And like her sister, Elinor finds that the role she plays gradually becomes a reality. She tells Marianne that: " 'The composure of mind with which I have brought myself at present to consider the matter [of Edward's engagement], the consolation that I have been willing to admit, have been the effect of constant and painful exertion;— they did not spring up of themselves;—they did not occur to relieve my spirits at first—No, Marianne" (p. 264). By behaving as if she could bear her grief calmly, Elinor has indeed developed the capacity to live with her sorrow. This does not mean that she has killed feeling—for she still loves Edward when she thinks he has married Lucy and would, probably, have remained true to his memory much longer than the impetuous, enthusiastic Marianne remained true to the memory of Willoughby, had his marriage with Lucy actually taken place [18]—but it does mean that her role-playing has had a strengthening effect upon her powers of control. The major rules of propriety suggest roles for conducting life's crucial relationships which, in this novel, are basically healthful to play, since they emphasize the values of restraint, stability, and duty, which combat the destructive power of feeling. These conventions are justified, as Elinor believes, simply because they work better than any practicable substitute.

With the constructive powers of feeling, *Sense and Sensibility,* unlike most of Jane Austen's later novels, is little concerned. Edward and Elinor, for example, are not (like Elizabeth and Darcy) brought together by the power of their love, but rather by the power of Lucy's ambition. The possibility that the conventional rules of propriety may repress good and constructive feelings is only very briefly considered in the novel. Elinor wants Marianne to conceal and try to retard the rapid progress of her love for Willoughby at the time when his behavior appears completely honorable—and at that time we cannot help being mostly on Marianne's side. But later it becomes apparent that even this positive emotion of love is suspect in the world of *Sense and Sensibility* because it contains within itself the possibility for destructive grief. In the absence of certainty even good emotions can turn sour—and in *Sense and Sensibility* they generally do (thus Marianne's love for Willoughby, Willoughby's for Marianne, Col. Brandon's for Eliza the first and for Marianne,

Eliza the second's for Willoughby, Edward's for Lucy, Elinor's for Edward, Edward's for Elinor, and so forth, all bring acute grief).

The ability to play the role of a sensibility heroine effectively is given to Marianne by her genuinely strong feelings, and the ability to play the role of control is given to Elinor by her genuinely strong sense of duty. Just as Elinor feels that it is her duty to protect the comfort of others by treating them with polite consideration, so she feels it is her duty to spare those who love her from witnessing her sufferings and to defend herself against the destructive ravages of feeling. The major rules of propriety, she finds, help her to achieve these ends fairly efficiently. Marianne is not naturally a self-regarding person, but her adherence to the cult of sensibility forces her to see the indulgence of her own feelings as the highest moral value. She is therefore compelled to ignore the suffering her role-playing causes her family. In choosing to follow feeling, which is basically self-regarding, Marianne rejects duty to others, which generally opposes desire. It is paradoxical, but undeniable, that in the world of *Sense and Sensibility,* to act only in accordance with personal desire is both selfish and self-destructive. For in this world where judgment is never certain, even the most selfish feelings are apt to want things that are essentially harmful to the self—thus Marianne's desire to play to the hilt the role of heroine nearly destroys her physically. After her illness, Marianne realizes that her behavior has exhibited consistent "imprudence toward myself and want of kindness to others" (p. 345). It is "imprudent," that is, unwise, for the self to forego the protection from the destructive powers of feeling that the major rules of propriety can provide. It is "unkind," that is, immoral and in violation of the social contract, to ignore the minor rules of propriety that define duty to others. Elinor has suspected this all along, but it is only at the end of the novel that Marianne finally accepts Elinor's original view that the rules of propriety, with all their drawbacks, really do represent something approaching a morally valid standard of social behavior. These rules are morally valid partially because they represent the terms of a fairly just and workable social contract, partially because the accumulated social wisdom they embody is reasonably efficient in protecting the individual from some of the most horrendous social consequences of uncertain judgment in a complex world.

In other novels Jane Austen is able to imagine a world in which feeling and duty to self and society generally coincide, but in *Sense and Sensibility* they typically oppose each other. Feeling here may follow duty, as Elinor's calmness follows her pretensions of indifference or as Marianne's love for Col. Brandon follows, "in time," her resolution of "entering on new duties" (p. 279) as his wife, but it follows painfully and at a distance. The code of propriety which *Sense and Sensibility* as a whole suggests is morally valid is a rule-oriented code, a code which places conventional ideas concerning duty to society and to self before the dictates of personal judgment and desire. Perhaps in a novel that is attacking the cult of sensibility, though not sensibility itself, this must be so, just as such a novel must, by its nature, emphasize the destructive powers of feeling above the constructive ones. One of Jane Austen's basic assumptions in *Sense and Sensibility* is that individual human judgments are essentially fallible and self-interested. Wisdom and morality (not perfect wisdom or perfect morality, but merely workable approximations) are most apt to reside in those collective and time-tested human judgments concerning the problems of social life that are embodied in the conventional rules of propriety.

The relationship of the intelligent and sensitive individual to a society composed, for the most part, of very inferior people, is a complex one in *Sense and Sensibility*. Surrounded by unpleasant social demands and by conventions of propriety that restrict his freedom of action and feeling, the individual cannot, as Marianne originally believes, remain a part of society yet sacrifice nothing of himself. Society is here conceived as a contractual arrangement in which benefits are exchanged for duties. One cannot withdraw unilaterally from this contract. In a sense, this is a game in which no one can win, for life in society necessarily involves, as Elinor painfully learns, adjusting oneself to the sadly low level of those with whom one must spend time and obeying rules of propriety which often pull against personal judgment and feeling. But the larger lesson of the novel is not quite so pessimistic. If it is a martyrdom to Elinor to have to spend days with Mrs. Jennings, it is still a martyrdom from which she learns something. In a world where judgment is highly uncertain, it is usually better to act in accordance with cautious convention than to run the risk of audacious error. If feeling and duty pull in opposite directions, it may be better to repress feeling—which so often proves destructive—and seek the less fickle, if colder, joys of conscience. And feeling, in any case, is so powerful that it is not going to disappear, no matter how forcefully it is governed by convention.[19] The rules of propriety are repressive and a person like

Elinor, who insists on following them to the letter, may place excessive stress on their less important purposes, such as the protection of privacy. But they are protective and helpful as well, for they provide individuals with generally workable ways of structuring their relationship to society, and in the sombre world of *Sense and Sensibility* the most intelligent individual, confronted as he is by the forces of selfishness, destructive feeling, and uncertain judgment, really needs their wisdom and protection.

# PROPRIETY
# AS A TEST
# OF CHARACTER:
# *PRIDE AND PREJUDICE*

In *Pride and Prejudice,* Jane Austen makes the basic assumption that a person's outward manners mirror his moral character. If, in this novel, a man or woman always displays good manners, it is perfectly safe for the reader to assume that his character is truly good. The characters in the novel continually try to evaluate one another's manners and the moral worth to which they are a clue. Often these evaluations are wrong, but it is important to note that they are never wrong because the manners of the individual in question have lied about his character. If an attempt to judge character from manners backfires in the world of *Pride and Prejudice,* it is invariably either because the judging individual has misperceived the nature of the manners of the individual he is judging, or because the standard of propriety according to which the judgment is being made is a mistaken one. The problem of judgment in *Pride and Prejudice* is not, as it is in *Persuasion,* for example, primarily a question of penetrating behind the facade of the manners to the reality of moral character; rather it is a question of perceiving and estimating the nature of an individual's manners with a reasonable degree of accuracy.

In a novel where a person's public manners are assumed to be an accurate clue to his private character, the definition of what truly proper manners actually are has an extraordinary importance. The reader must be convinced that the standard of propriety in question is one to which intelligent people of good feeling can give their wholehearted adherence. Jane Austen, it seems to me, achieves this aim in *Pride and Prejudice.* Elizabeth Bennet's standards of decorous behavior do not grate upon the reader's sensibilities as, for example, Elinor Dashwood's excessively rigid and stoical conception of propriety sometimes does.[1] Yet Elizabeth's standards of propriety, at least at the close of the novel, are being presented as identical to the best standards of proper behavior held by her society, as well as identical to the standards of the novel as a whole—and so conformist an ethic might be expected to offend modern readers.

Jane Austen manages to get her readers—even most of her twentieth-century readers—to approve Elizabeth's adherence to a socially acceptable standard of propriety by employing a variety of subtly concealed persuasive techniques. The definition of true propriety which *Pride and Prejudice* offers—to anticipate somewhat—is simply a healthy respect for the conventional rules of social behavior, modified by an understanding that those forms are important, not as ends in themselves, but as means of regulating social intercourse, and that therefore they need not always be followed slavishly.

Jane Austen here seems to be dividing rules of propriety into two classes: those rules that represent the social codification of basic moral principles, and those that are primarily matters of fashion or convenience. This division does not correspond to the division of propriety into minor rules (governing everyday social interaction) and major rules (governing the handling of the most important social and familial relationships, as well as behavior in crucial and dangerous social situations) that is important in *Sense and Sensibility*. All the major rules, in terms of *Sense and Sensibility*'s division, clearly fall within the class of basically moral rules in terms of *Pride and Prejudice*'s division. However, the minor rules, considered in *Sense and Sensibility* as a unit, are divided in *Pride and Prejudice* between the class of basically moral minor rules and the class of minor rules that are merely matters of convenience. As we shall see in the following chapters, an example of a minor rule that is basically moral in character is the rule against breaking a first engagement because one has received a second invitation. An example of a minor rule that is a matter of fashion or convenience only is the rule prohibiting young ladies from taking long country walks by themselves. The implication in *Pride and Prejudice* is that people of true propriety always respect both major and minor rules of propriety which have an important moral element because it would be immoral to do otherwise, but respect rules that are matters of fashion and convenience only where they seem to be reasonably functional and sensible (in practice this turns out to be most of the time). The validity of those rules of propriety which have an important moral element (a class which includes all the major rules as they are defined in *Sense and Sensibility,* as well as many minor rules) is not seriously questioned in this novel.

The first aspect of this definition of propriety—that individuals ought generally to respect the conventional rules of social behavior, especially where those rules have a significant moral element—is a tacit assumption in *Pride and Prejudice.* Jane Austen does not state this idea overtly, perhaps because she senses that the bald statement of so conformist a norm might alienate some readers and, at any rate, could hardly be found novel or intriguing, but she enforces it vigorously, nonetheless, by using all her charm as a humorous writer to lure her readers into participating in her censure of *all* those characters who fail to respect the conventional forms of decorum. *Pride and Prejudice* contains no character, like Mrs. Jennings or Admiral Croft, whose impropriety of behavior is actually a clue to internal worth—Mrs. Jennings's impertinent curiosity, in fact, indicating, at least in part, her warm and generous interest in other people, Admiral Croft's impulsiveness indicating exuberant good feeling—so that the reader, whether he realizes it or not, is being manipulated into feeling that the forms of propriety are very desirable. Indeed, Jane Austen is very careful, in *Pride and Prejudice,* to give her readers precise characterizations of the manners of most of her important characters very close to their first appearances in the novel, and perhaps one of her reasons for following this rather uncharacteristic procedure is her desire to make absolutely sure that her readers do not begin by making the erroneous assumption that unattractive characters like Miss Bingley can ever have really well-bred manners (and thus we get fairly accurate descriptions of Bingley's manners, pp. 10, 14, 16, Darcy's manners, pp. 10, 16, Miss Bingley and Mrs. Hurst's manners, p. 15, Sir William Lucas's manners, p. 18, Elizabeth's manners, p. 23, Jane's manners, p. 21, and so forth).

However, Jane Austen is much more explicit in defining the second aspect of her idea of true propriety in this novel: that is, her belief that all the forms of propriety are there for a purpose (be that purpose basically moral or basically a matter of social convenience) and hence are being perverted if they are treated as ends in themselves. The incident of Elizabeth's solitary three-mile walk to Netherfield, which occurs very early in the novel, embodies the views on the purpose of the forms of decorum which the novel as a whole enforces, in a clear and unambiguous way. Jane Bennet, who has been visiting Netherfield, has fallen ill there and Elizabeth "feeling really anxious was determined to go to her, though the carriage was not to be had; and as she was no horsewoman, walking was her only alternative" (p. 32). The situation here is thus set up most plainly. Elizabeth has a very valid reason for wishing to go to Netherfield (we learn later that Jane "longed for such a visit" [p. 33]), and walking is her only means of getting there. Readers are obviously meant to feel that the rules of propriety prohibiting solitary cross-country hikes for young ladies—rules which are concerned with the neatness of the lady's appearance [2] and the possible danger to her consequent upon making a practice of walking long distances alone—ought rationally to be set aside in this unusual situation. In taking a three-mile walk, Elizabeth, as she is well aware, breaks no moral law.[3] And in fact, by their reactions to this crucial and unambiguous decision on a point of decorum, Jane Austen allows several of her characters to reveal what sort of stuff they are made of. " 'You will not be fit to be seen when you get there' " (p. 32), cries Mrs. Bennet, proving once again both that she has no idea of what is really important in social behavior and that she regards her daughter as merchandise on display. " 'Every impulse of feeling should be guided by reason . . . exertion should always be in proportion to what is required' " (p. 32), says Mary Bennet, revealing the fact that she completely fails to understand what is required by Elizabeth's love for Jane. " 'We will go as far as Meryton with you' " (p. 32), say Kitty and Lydia, uninterested in theoretical questions of propriety in the heat of their own headlong pursuit of officers. " 'It seems to me to show . . . a most country-town indifference to decorum' " (p. 36), says Miss Bingley, a social climber who values herself on the elegance and fashion of her own behavior, which, however, is often contemptuous and rude. The good-natured, unpretentious Bingley is able to see that Elizabeth's walk "shows an affection for her sister that is very pleasing" (p. 36). And Mr. Darcy, admiring "the brilliancy which exercize had given [Elizabeth's] complexion," but doubting "the occasion's justifying her coming so far alone" (p. 33) reveals both a basic understanding of what good manners are and a characteristic tendency to place too much stress on preserving the forms of gentility, a tendency that results from pride in his own high social status. Thus, the incident of Elizabeth's walk defines explicitly what might be called the functional aspect of the *Pride and Prejudice* ideal of propriety and smaller incidents of similar import later in the novel—such as the one in which Elizabeth defends the right of younger sisters to come out socially before the elder ones are married—prevent the reader from forgetting the point.

By failing to live up to the novel's ideal of propriety—a respect for the conventions of propriety modified by an understanding that those conventions are not ends in themselves—or by revealing the fact that their concept of proper behavior differs from that suggested by the novel as a whole, the characters in *Pride and Prejudice* reveal their own moral shortcomings. And it is not merely that something vaguely wrong with the manners is a clue to something vaguely wrong with the character, for in fact the flaw in the manners usually turns out to be a very precise counterpart to the moral flaw in question. A significant example of the way this concept works can be seen in the character of Charlotte Lucas. Charlotte is a sensible, well-meaning young woman, and her manners are generally polite and unaffected. In fact, Charlotte is guilty of only one real breach of propriety in the course of the novel, but this breach is very significant, for it provides an unambiguous clue to the moral flaw which will eventually cause Charlotte to marry Mr. Collins and become the sycophantic dependent of Lady Catherine de Bourgh. Charlotte arrives to visit the Bennet family immediately after Elizabeth has refused Mr. Collins's proposal of marriage. As she is sitting with Mrs. Bennet and the girls, Mr. Collins enters, and on perceiving him, Mrs. Bennet says, " 'Now I do insist upon it that you, all of you . . . let Mr. Collins and me have a little conversation together' " (p. 113). Elizabeth, Jane, and even Kitty "passed quietly out of the room" at this request, but Charlotte "detained at first by the civility of Mr. Collins . . . and then by a little curiosity, satisfied herself by walking to the window and pretending not to hear" (p. 114). In fact, Charlotte eavesdrops on the whole conversation and this tiny incident contains the key to Charlotte's character. Elizabeth and Jane, with their delicate sense of personal honor, would consider it beneath them to eavesdrop on any conversation, however interesting.[4] But Charlotte is perfectly willing to satisfy her curiosity (which, of course, reveals her interest in Mr. Collins) in this underhand way, for it is the fault of her character that she lacks firm principle and the sense of personal integrity that make one obey one's conscience when it dictates the sacrifice of personal advantage. Thus, by this minor act of impropriety, Charlotte reveals the traits which will later make it possible for her to violate principle in order to marry, for security, a man she does not love and to court, for advancement, a woman she cannot respect. A woman who marries Mr. Collins, says Elizabeth, " 'cannot have a proper way of thinking . . . though it is Charlotte Lucas!' " (p. 135) and it is precisely her improper way of thinking that Charlotte's improper manners would have demonstrated to Elizabeth, had Elizabeth observed those manners more closely.

And as Charlotte's manners reveal her character flaw so precisely, so do the manners of virtually all the other characters in the novel. Sir William Lucas and Mr. Collins are both, in different ways, so enamored of the forms of civility that the purpose of those forms has largely been forgotten. Sir William occupies "himself solely in being civil to all the world" (p. 18), hardly a worthy lifetime occupation. Mr. Collins has fallen deeply in love with two of the commonest forms of politeness—the apology and the thank you—and has completely failed to understand that those forms have definite functions in social intercourse. Thus, he bestows his thanks liberally on people who have absolutely no claim to his gratitude—as when he thanks Lady Catherine "for every fish he won" from her at cards (p. 166). And, by the same token, he apologizes when he cannot possibly have offended—at cards again "apologizing" to Lady Catherine "if he thought he won too many [fish]" (p. 166). The fact that both these characters are so concerned with empty forms of propriety reveals both their empty heads and their purposeless lives. Another group of characters misunderstand or ignore the forms of politeness in various ways. Mrs. Bennet addresses those who please her "with a degree of civility which made her two daughters ashamed" (p. 355), but is frankly rude to anyone who crosses her, and this inconsistency of manners is just one more example of Mrs. Bennet's characteristic tendency to judge and react to things entirely as they affect her as an individual, completely disregarding any function they may serve in the world as a whole. " 'I do think it is the hardest thing in the world that your estate should be entailed away from your own children; and I am sure if I had been you I should have tried long ago to do something or other about it,' " she tells her husband (p. 62). Good manners to Mrs. Bennet are just one more way of getting what she wants, and she has failed to teach her daughters Kitty and Lydia, "always unguarded and often uncivil" (p. 126), anything at all about the importance or function of decorous behavior. Lydia's tendency to ignore the rules of propriety without thinking anything much about them is the clue to her more serious decision to ignore the rules of morality in living with a man who has not married her ("she was sure they would be married sometime or other and it did not much signify when" [p. 323]). Lydia ignores both propriety and morality in an unthinking pursuit of personal satisfaction. Miss Bingley and Mrs. Hurst "were in the habit . . . of associating with people of rank. . . . They were of a respectable family . . . a circumstance more deeply impressed on their memories than that their brother's fortune and their own had been acquired by trade" (p. 15). They hope to succeed with the nobility and place a good deal of stress on elegance and fashion in manners, but they reveal their lack of true gentility in their willingness to be rude to social inferiors like Elizabeth. Lady Catherine's dictatorial and condescending manners toward those she considers socially inferior reveal her pride of rank as well as the fact that she is uninterested in judging people by their inherent worth. Mr. Bennet's manners are in a class by themselves, for he is clever enough to be able to pervert the forms of politeness—which he, unlike the characters discussed above, thoroughly understands—into a weapon which he uses against those whom he despises. " 'My dear,' " he says to Mrs. Bennet, masking insult under the forms of courtesy, " 'I have two small favors to request. First, that you will allow me the free use of my understanding on the present occasion; and secondly, of my room. I shall be glad to have the library to myself as soon as may be' " (p. 112)—an offensively polite way of saying shut up and get out. Thus Mr. Bennet makes the forms of politeness serve the purposes of his contempt for others. And in a similar manner Mr. Bennet perverts his considerable talents ("talents which rightly used, might at least have preserved the respectability of his daughters" [p. 237]), using them not to serve any desirable end, but merely to increase his idle amusement at the follies of a family to which he should have taught better behavior.[5]

Many other examples could be given of the way in which manners mirror the moral character in the world of *Pride and Prejudice,* for this is true of nearly every character in the novel. And this is an important difference between *Sense and Sensibility* and *Pride and Prejudice.* In *Sense and Sensibility,* the rules of propriety are ultimately justified by their connection with the concept of duty—and true propriety consists of following them to the letter, even when they oppose personal judgment and feeling. This is a very exacting and theoretical standard of propriety and perhaps that is why Jane Austen does not assume that to fall below this high standard is invariably evidence of real immorality. Thus, Mrs. Jennings's frequent improprieties are signs that she has not always lived in good society and that her friendly interest in others is sometimes carried to an uncomfortable pitch—but not that she is in any sense a bad person. Mrs. Jennings does not have Elinor's sophisticated understanding of the function of a code of propriety in the social system, but she can still be a good woman in her less stoical and intellectual way. Also, since the external manifestation of *Sense and Sensibility*'s code of true propriety consists simply of obeying all the major and minor rules of propriety to the letter, it can easily be followed by those unfeeling, unintelligent people, like Lady Middleton, who have few personal desires or judgments urging them to disobey. But *Pride and Prejudice*'s standard of propriety suggests that the truly proper individual must disobey the rules whenever sound common sense and good morality approve—so that only people possessing these two important attributes *can* live up to the novel's ideal of propriety, even in a purely external sense. That is why improper characters must be either immoral or stupid in *Pride and Prejudice,* but not in *Sense and Sensibility*.

And, as one might expect, this idea of manners as an outward manifestation of inward moral value plays an important role in the main theme of the novel: Elizabeth's proud and prejudiced misjudgment of Darcy and Wickham. In tracing how Elizabeth's misjudgment of Darcy and Wickham's manners contributes to her misjudgment of their characters, we shall see that manners mirror character so closely in *Pride and Prejudice* that the problem of judgment is reduced almost entirely to a problem of evaluating outward social manners. Darcey's relationship with Elizabeth begins in an act which she perceives as an act of rudeness. At the first Meryton ball attended by Bingley's party, Bingley suggests that Darcey, who is not dancing, stand up with Elizabeth. " 'Which do you mean?' " asks Darcey, "and turning round, he looked for a moment at Elizabeth, til catching her eye, he withdrew his own and coldly said, 'She is tolerable, but not handsome enough to tempt me; and I am in no humor at present to give consequence to young ladies who are slighted by other men' " (p. 13).

Elizabeth, needless to say, is not pleased with this comment, which implies that she is both unattractive and unpopular, and she views the remark as a definite piece of rudeness. But the mere fact that her mother shares this view—for Mrs. Bennet later "related with much bitterness of spirit and some exaggeration, the shocking rudeness of

Mr. Darcy" (p. 13) to her husband—ought to make us suspicious. And, in fact, when examined more closely, Darcy's remark, though certainly not good-natured or friendly, need not be seen as actually rude. For Darcy, after all, has been rudely insulting to Elizabeth only if he intended her to overhear his remark, and on this point we have no evidence (except that his withdrawing his eye on catching Elizabeth's may indicate that he didn't want her to notice his observation). Conversations in crowded rooms are frequently overheard in Jane Austen's novels. Given Jane Austen's passion for verisimilitude of detail, we can probably assume that she would not have used this device repeatedly if she were not convinced that people are often unaware how far their voices can carry through a crowd buzzing with conversation, to the ears of an alert, interested listener.[6] Possible, Darcy *is* unaware that Elizabeth has been watching him with great interest and is listening sharply enough to catch tones which he assumes are inaudible to her. At this very same Meryton ball, we later learn, Charlotte Lucas, who likes to overhear things, has overheard Mr. Robinson ask Bingley "Whether he did not think there were a great many pretty women in the room, and *which* he thought the prettiest? and his answering immediately to the last question—Oh! the eldest Miss Bennet without a doubt, there cannot be two opinions on that point" (p. 19). Now one might validly consider it rude for Mr. Robinson and Mr. Bingley to discuss Jane Bennet's superior charms in Charlotte's hearing, but Charlotte is not vain of her looks and the Bennet family is pleased that Bingley admires Jane, so no one even thinks to accuse these gentlemen of rudeness. But readers are obviously meant to contrast this incident with the almost simultaneous one in which Elizabeth overhears Mr. Darcy—"'*My* overhearings were more to the purpose than *yours,* Eliza'" (p. 19), says Charlotte, underlining the similarity— and to conclude that the Bennets are not completely justified in their belief that Darcy has been very rude to Elizabeth, and that they have jumped to that conclusion primarily because the overheard remark was so unflattering in nature. Darcy's remark certainly indicates that his character is seriously flawed. It is ungracious, snobbish, and shows a desire to think poorly of others, but it does not necessarily show (as Elizabeth believes) a willingness to break important, morally oriented rules of propriety, like the rule that one should not wound others by openly displaying contempt for them.

Elizabeth chooses to view Darcey's remark as an act of rudeness, and until the revelation of his true character in the middle of the novel, she continues to interpret his least offensive behavior as in-civility. And, in fact, Jane Austen is extremely careful to show her readers that after the remark at the ball—which may or may not have been intentionally rude—Darcy's behavior to Elizabeth is not invariably gracious, but at least invariably polite. When Sir William, whose too civil manners are always embarrassing, distresses Eliza-beth by offering her to Mr. Darcy as a dancing partner, Darcy requests the honor of her hand "with grave propriety" (p. 26) which entirely escapes her notice. When Mrs. Hurst and Miss Bingley openly slight Elizabeth at Netherfield, "Mr. Darcy felt their rude-ness" (p. 53) and tried to remedy it, though Elizabeth once again ignored him. He addresses Jane on her recovery from a bad cold "with a polite congratulation" (p. 54), and makes "polite inquiries" (p. 89) of Elizabeth at the Netherfield ball. But Elizabeth's opinion of Darcy's manners has been fixed on the basis of his first ambiguous slight, so that when he asks her to dance a reel, she is certain he wishes to despise her taste, and when he watches her playing and singing, is sure he is rudely trying to alarm her. From the first, she tells him later, "your manners impressing me with the fullest belief of . . . your selfish disdain of the feelings of others, were such as to form that groundwork of disapprobation, on which succeeding events have built so immovable a dislike" (p. 193). Elizabeth, notic-ing only Darcy's ungraciousness, sees his manners as selfish and rude, when Jane Austen is at pains to show her readers that those manners are often awkward and cold, but consistently polite.

But Elizabeth thinks that Darcey's manners are rude and that his rudeness indicates both a lack of respect for others and a lack of moral principle. She believes Wickham's slander of Darcy in part because she believes that Darcy does openly violate the important, morally oriented laws of propriety—and she reasons that one who violates the dictates of this sort of law of propriety is very likely to violate the dictates of pure morality also, even to the point of dis-regarding a clause in his father's will leaving a living to a man he dislikes. And, as we have seen, this is a perfectly valid way to reason in the world of *Pride and Prejudice*—Elizabeth's reasoning here does precisely apply to her sister Lydia, though it is unfair to Darcy. Elizabeth is wrong about Darcy, not because his manners lie about his character, but because she has misperceived those man-ners. Darcy is, in fact, quite polite in a formal sense (even if we are unwilling to assume from his decorous behavior afterwards that he did not really intend Elizabeth to overhear his remark at the ball, still this is his only possible act of true impropriety), and what Elizabeth repeatedly identifies as real rudeness is actually something quite different: an ungraciousness of manner resulting mainly from an excessive sense of social and personal superiority. When Darcy, at the end of the novel, tells Elizabeth that " 'I was taught what was right, but I was not taught to correct my temper. I was given good principles, but left to follow them in pride and conceit' " (p. 369), he gives an accurate description of what his manners originally were. Convinced of his own superiority—and, incidentally, also shy—Darcy preferred despising his acquaintances to taking the trouble of getting to know them, but he never lacked respect—as Elizabeth thought—for the sensible and moral conventions of decorum and to be strictly well-mannered was always an important part of his self-image. The narrator, accurately as it turns out, remarks that his manners "though well-bred, were not inviting" (p. 16). Elizabeth's basic mistake in her estimate of Darcy's character was her conclusion that because he hurt her feelings, he was being intentionally rude to her and that therefore his manners were of the ill-bred sort that indicate a basically flawed moral character. Elizabeth's misperception of Darcy's character is thus integrally related to her misperception of his manners.

Just as an affront to her pride produces Elizabeth's prejudiced and distorted view of Darcy's manners, so Wickham's flattering behavior to her at the very opening of her acquaintance with him, leads Elizabeth to misjudge radically the nature of his manners and hence of his moral character. When Elizabeth first meets Wickham, she is already fairly well-acquainted with Mr. Darcy and has formed her low opinion of his manners and morals. Wickham's fabricated tale of Darcy's unprincipled behavior toward him therefore confirms an opinion to which Elizabeth is already emotionally committed, and hence she wishes—though she does not quite realize it—to credit Wickham's story. Further, the fact that Wickham tells his intimate story to her, a stranger, and to her alone, flatters Elizabeth. It is naturally more pleasing to Elizabeth to view Wickham's confidences to her as a discerning compliment not only to her attractiveness, but also to her obvious intelligence and discretion—for, after all, she *can* be trusted not to spread rumors—than it is for her to regard these confidences as secrets which it is categorically improper to relate to a stranger under any circumstances. Therefore, Elizabeth, though she is unaware of this fact, has a substantial emotional interest in believing Wickham's story and since believing his story necessarily involves believing in Wickham's character, Elizabeth must persuade herself that Wickham's manners, as a clue to his character, are well-bred and unexceptionable.[7]

Wickham's manners are, in fact, superficially polished and charming. On first seeing him, Elizabeth notes his "gentlemanlike appearance . . . and very pleasing address . . . perfectly correct and unassuming" (p. 72). The narrator does not set the reader straight concerning the true nature of Wickham's manners (as she does with Darcy), but Wickham's behavior quickly reveals to the reader, if not to the already prejudiced Elizabeth, that his manners are not really so gentlemanlike as they at first appear. In his first long conversation with Elizabeth about Darcy's character, Wickham's behavior is improper in the extreme. Such communications about the son of his benefactor should never, of course, be made to an absolute stranger. Wickham is well aware of this and tries to defend himself against possible charges of impropriety and ingratitude by asserting that he would never do the very thing that he is in fact doing. " 'Til I can forget [Mr. Darcy's] father, I can never defy or expose him' " (p. 80), he tells Elizabeth in the midst of his very complete exposé of Darcy's supposed inhumanity to him. Elizabeth herself is prevented by her instinctive sense of personal honor from asking Wickham any questions about Darcy, realizing that "the delicacy of [the subject] prevented farther inquiry" (p. 78), but she fails to reflect that a subject on which it is improper to make inquiries is probably one which should not be discussed at all. Wickham's manners on this occasion mirror his most basic character flaws. For his impropriety actually reveals the lack of respect for the important rules of decorum and the moral principles which stand behind those rules that Elizabeth wrongly thought she perceived in Darcy. And "the inconsistency of his professions with his conduct" (p. 207) reveals Wickham's fundamental hypocrisy. Thus Wickham's basically bad moral character has been obvious in his manners from the beginning, as Elizabeth realizes after reading Darcy's justification of his conduct to Wickham. "She was *now* struck with the impropriety of such communications to a stranger and wondered it had escaped her before" (p. 207). And Elizabeth is later able to realize, too, that the warmth and gentleness that always mark Wickham's manners are sometimes very inappropriate to the situations in which he is involved. Elizabeth is convinced that one ought to judge other people on the basis of individual worth, uninfluenced by any considerations of social status. She originally regards Darcy's invariable hauteur as a sign that he has rejected all Meryton society for purely snobbish reasons and sees Wickham's warmth as a generous response to real merit. But ultimately Elizabeth realizes that just as Darcy's excessive stiffness is mistaken and offensive, so in Wickham's invariable gentleness there is a "sameness to disgust and weary" (p. 233), and when Wickham behaves warmly and affectionately to the family of the girl he has seduced and married only under the inducement of bribery, Elizabeth realizes that dignity and suitability to the occasion are much more important elements in good manners than warm responsiveness.

Wickham's manners on the occasion of his first long talk with Elizabeth are very bad, but afterwards they become even more obviously improper, for he abruptly drops Elizabeth to pay court to a young lady who has suddenly acquired £10,000 and of whom he had not taken the slightest notice prior to that event. Elizabeth's emotional commitment to her belief in Wickham's good character is such, however, that she undertakes to convince herself that her friend's manners are at all times unexceptionable, that he is always "her model of the amiable and pleasing" (p. 152). And in her attempt to convince herself that Wickham's bad manners are really good manners, Elizabeth is forced to distort her own conception of propriety to the point where it becomes invalid. Elizabeth, as we have seen, is originally a sensible advocate for a mild degree of individual discretion on minor questions of decorum. She thinks that minor rules of propriety which are merely matters of fashion or convenience may sometimes be violated,[8] but she does not by any means condone violating rules of propriety that are closely connected with moral principles. She is also a believer in human relationships based on mutual esteem. So when Wickham makes his improper confidences to her, Elizabeth's pleasure in the intimacy they have established makes her justify to herself as reasonable and sensible what is actually an unjustifiable breach of propriety. And when Wickham pays his attentions to the newly rich Miss King, Elizabeth fails to reflect—as she justly did when Charlotte accepted Mr. Collins—that it is immoral to marry solely for money and truly indecorous to pursue a woman merely because she has suddenly become wealthy. In fact, when her aunt, Mrs. Gardiner, points out the "indelicacy" (p. 153) of Wickham's behavior, Elizabeth replies that "'A man in distressed circumstances has not time for all those elegant decorums which other people may observe'" (p. 153). We must recall Elizabeth's walk to Netherfield—an occasion on which she showed herself willing to break a minor law of decorum for a very worthy and valid motive—to realize how Elizabeth's concept of good breeding has become coarsened and falsified under the stress of her need to believe in Wickham's good manners and character. Here she classes what is, in fact, a law of decorum with a vital moral element—that a man should not court a rich girl for whom he obviously does not care at all—with the sort of rule of decorum, like the one prohibiting solitary female walking, that is entirely a matter of fashion and convenience. In her desire to justify Wickham, Elizabeth has confused the moral and fashionable aspects of propriety and has moved to an unjustifiably libertarian concept of manners.[9]

When Darcy's explanatory letter finally opens Elizabeth's eyes to Wickham's true character and the need to justify his behavior disappears, Elizabeth understands the mistakes into which she has fallen and is horrified. When her unprincipled sister Lydia remarks without censure that Wickham had never cared about the "nasty, little, freckled" (p. 220) Miss King, "Elizabeth was shocked to think that . . . the coarseness of the *sentiment* was little other than her own breast had formerly harbored and fancied liberal" (p. 220). So Elizabeth reverts to something like her original view of the nature of good manners, and the only change is that she now places a somewhat greater stress on the importance of conventional propriety than before. It is after she realizes the error of her libertarian views that Elizabeth becomes deeply concerned about the impropriety of behavior that has characterized her own family. Previously this impropriety had embarrassed Elizabeth, but she had not regarded it as very important.[10] But now she considers it most seriously and even takes the rather remarkable step (remarkable because, in the world of Jane Austen, even very deficient parents invariably receive scrupulous outward respect) of advising her father that it is his duty to attempt to correct "Lydia's unguarded and imprudent manner" (p. 231). Further, she is now able to realize that, though Darcy's manners have lacked graciousness, the strict propriety which has generally marked them is most valuable as evidence of sound and firm moral values.

And as Elizabeth's manners become more formal, Darcy's manners are also changing. He is shocked by Elizabeth's charge that his manners are not "gentlemanlike" (p. 192) and decides that she is at least partially correct ("'My behavior . . . merited the severest reproof'" [p. 367]). Darcy censures himself for the stiff and haughty manners that reveal his wish "'to think meanly of all the rest of the world,' " on very insufficient evidence (p. 369). When he encounters Elizabeth at Pemberley, Darcy is determined to show her that his manners now exhibit true consideration for others, as well as merely formal politeness. His behavior at Pemberley to her socially inferior merchant relatives, the Gardiners, as Mrs. Gardiner herself remarks, was " 'more than civil, it was really attentive; and there was no necessity for such attention' " (p. 257) according to the ordinary rules of propriety. By his considerate and polite manners toward the Gardiners, Darcy shows both that his worst character flaw—the desire to look down on other people, particularly those of lower status—and his overly formal concept of propriety, have been corrected.[11] Meanwhile, Elizabeth has mended her own tendency to disregard the strict rules of propriety a bit too readily (" 'my behavior to *you* was at least always bordering on the uncivil' " [p. 380]). So both she and Darcy move closer to the ideal of propriety enforced by the novel as a whole—principled respect for the rules of decorum, combined with an intelligent realization that merely to obey the rules in their strictest sense does not constitute the whole of good breeding—as they move closer to each other.

It seems paradoxical that *Pride and Prejudice,* probably Jane Austen's most popular novel and certainly the one that gives readers the greatest sense of the individual's right to be different,[12] is the only one of Jane Austen's books, except for *Northanger Abbey,* that assumes a simple, direct relationship between conventional good manners and good moral character. It is precisely because Jane Austen manages to convince her readers, in this novel, that the laws of morality manifest themselves socially in terms of the laws of propriety—an association that is made linguistically again and again in the course of *Pride and Prejudice:* "folly and indecorum" (p. 236), "decency and virtue" (p. 283), and so forth—that we can accept the idea that her most attractive characters choose socially conventional modes of behavior freely, as a means of realizing their best potentialities. Perhaps part of the charm of *Pride and Prejudice* is to be found in the way it subtly convinces readers that what the intelligent individual wants for himself and what society wants him to be are virtually one and the same, that Elizabeth Bennet is free to be Elizabeth in the best sense, and, in addition, to be the ideal mistress of Pemberley.

# PROPRIETY AND THE EDUCATION OF CATHERINE MORLAND: *NORTHANGER ABBEY*

*Northanger Abbey* is, in part, a spoof of gothic and sentimental novels.[1] But its main action—the realistically drawn picture of an unformed young girl's education in the complexities of real life—can be fairly easily detached from the elements of literary burlesque with which it is surrounded and discussed on its own terms. By tracing the development of Catherine Morland's character we can discover that her misconceptions about the true nature and value of proper manners play a role in her most serious errors of judgment. Since the nature and significance of the literary allusions Jane Austen makes in *Northanger Abbey* have been intelligently and, in my opinion, exhaustively discussed by other critics, I intend to mention them here only insofar as they are relevant to the real adventures of that believable human being, Catherine Morland, whose growing up is one of the main subjects of *Northanger Abbey*. Literature plays a part in Catherine's education, as it does in that of so many other Jane Austen heroines, but to approach the novel as primarily a literary satire tends to force the reader to overestimate the importance of burlesque elements in Catherine's characterization. I hope to demonstrate here that literature does not, in fact, play the central role in the learning process which the ignorant Catherine must undergo if she is to cope effectively with the rigors of adult life.

At the beginning of *Northanger Abbey*, Catherine is unformed, but it would be a mistake to consider her as a mere tabula rasa. In the course of the novel, a number of scattered references are made to the nature of Catherine's family and to the sort of upbringing she has been given. If we combine the bits of evidence with which we are provided in these references, we can form a fairly adequate idea of the sort of sheltered world Catherine has known before her introduction into the wider and more perilous society of Bath. It is, of course, from the world of her childhood that Catherine has drawn the opinions concerning manners, morals, and human nature with which she will evaluate the new society she is entering.

Perhaps the most significant thing which we learn about Catherine at the opening of the novel is that she is "as free from the apprehension of evil as from the knowledge of it" (p. 237). The neighborhood of Catherine's home at Fullerton parsonage apparently has provided her with only a very small circle of intimate acquaintances and those mostly of the best moral character. Her own parents are sensible, unpretentious, modest, generous, and well-bred. They are, in fact, "plain, matter-of-fact people, who seldom aimed at wit of any kind; her father, at the utmost, being contented with a pun, and her mother with a proverb; they were not in the habit therefore of telling lies to increase their importance" (pp. 65–66). Outside of her own immediate family, Catherine's only close friends are the Allens. When in search of amusement in the country, Catherine tells Henry Tilney, " 'I can only go and call on Mrs. Allen' " (p. 79). " 'What a picture of intellectual poverty,' " Henry replies (p. 79), and he is certainly right. For Mrs. Allen, as Jane Austen takes pains to point out, is a veritable cipher of a woman, "one of that numerous class of females whose society can raise no other emotion than surprise at their being any men in the world who could like them well enough to marry them" (p. 20). And Mr. Allen is just such another plain and unpretentious man as Catherine's own father. We can conclude Catherine's other acquaintances to be neither numerous, nor intimate. Unlike Isabella Thorpe, Catherine mention no old friends by name. And we learn that not one family in the neighborhood of Fullerton has a son of anything like the proper age for becoming Catherine's lover. All this suggests a very restricted society.

It seems safe to conclude, then, that Catherine's limited circle of acquaintances has provided her with several examples of unpretending merit, but has given her virtually no first-hand knowledge of evil in any of its human forms. One of the most important things that is going to happen to Catherine in the course of *Northanger Abbey* is her encounter with evil. She must discover for herself the characteristic ways in which human evil manifests itelf in polite English society. In this task the experiences of her early life can help Catherine in only two possible ways. First, she can hope to recognize evil by its contrast with the sort of goodness she has previously known. Second, she can trust to the experiences of a wider world than that of Fullerton, which her reading has vicariously given her, as a guide in understanding the new types of people she will encounter at Bath. For Catherine is a reader. We learn that before going to Bath, Catherine has read some history, which she dislikes, some Pope, some Gray, some Thompson, and some Shakespeare, plus Richardson's *Sir Charles Grandison,* entire. This list is rather impressive and there can be no doubt that the quality of Catherine's literary fare drops sharply when Isabella Thorpe begins recommending her own favorite novels. On Isabella's advice, Catherine switches from Richardson to the genteel gothic fiction of Mrs. Radcliffe. She is, apparently, also planning to read several books by imitators of the sensational gothic novelist, "Monk" Lewis. We might hope that Catherine's earlier reading of respectable authors as provided her with ideas that will prove useful in evaluating the varied society of Bath, but Jane Austen makes it clear that Catherine's reading has been of a desultory and light-hearted nature and cannot be expected to supply anything "serviceable" in dealing with the "vissisitudes" (p. 15) of her new life. It is, as we shall see later, only the reading in gothic novels which Catherine does *after* she reaches Bath, that remains fresh enough in the young heroine's mind to be drawn upon for aid in understanding and interpreting her unprecedented experiences of evil. The didactic literature of which Mrs. Morland is fond (*Grandison* is her favorite, and she is impressed by *The Mirror*'s instructive essays) has made little or no lasting impression on her daughter. And this probably represents Jane Austen's considered opinion of the educational value of didactic fiction for the average young mind.[2]

Catherine's experiences before she goes to Bath, then, have not taught her how to deal with people who are selfish, vain, pretentious, and improper in their social behavior. Her first acquaintance with such people is in Bath. Her first reaction to such people is characterized by her failure to realize that they are different from people whom she has previously known. Catherine's own family are completely without pretensions to being anything other than ordinary people; they do not affect to rise above "the common feelings of common life" (p. 19). Their manners are conventionally proper, their understanding of reality quite adequate to the demands of everyday life. There is no need for Catherine to take her parents at anything other than their face value and for a long time she fails to realize that the world is full of pretentious and affected people who cannot be accepted at their own estimates of themselves. Indeed, an excessive willingness to believe what people say of themselves remains a part of Catherine's character throughout the novel, and this trait is moderated, rather than completely cured, by her experiences.

Catherine first encounters human evil, which in *Northanger Abbey* typically takes the form of selfishness, vanity, pretension, and impropriety, in the persons of Isabella and John Thorpe. It immediately becomes clear to the reader that both John and Isabella have absolutely no feeling for others and no commitment to truth of any sort. They are also greedy and financially ambitious. In *Northanger Abbey,* as in *Pride and Prejudice,* a man's manners are seen as the social manifestations of his moral condition. Manners here reveal, rather than conceal (as is partially the case in *Persuasion,* for example), the reality of character. And the manners of the Thorpes mirror their characters perfectly. They are both pretentious, but too shallow and foolish to ground their pretensions on any solid undestanding of reality, and John and Isabella betray both their dishonesty and their inability to understand the real world in their manners. Neither has much understanding of even the minor rules of propriety governing ordinary social interaction. Both create their own idiosyncratic codes of propriety designed to meet the needs of their overweening egos. Thus John Thorpe "seemed fearful of being . . . too much like a gentleman unless he were easy where he ought to be civil, and impudent where he might be allowed to be easy" (p. 45). In other words, John disregards all the ordinary, minor rules of civility in order to prove to himself and to others that he is in command of any social situation. John's disregard of conventional decorum when it conflicts with his own ends extends to the major, as well as the minor, rules of propriety. He is quite prepared to lie about both trivial and very important matters at any time and doesn't even have the sense to be disturbed when he is found out. The rule of propriety which prohibits lying (whether in everyday social relations or where something crucially important is concerned) is a very basic and significant one, resting virtually on the line where conventional propriety and pure morality merge. Yet John ignores it openly and repeatedly, telling lies which are sure to be found out about even the most significant aspects of social relations. And this is the outward evidence that he has absolutely no idea of what is important in social behavior, either from the point of view of mere social acceptability or from that of morality. He is beyond the pale.

Isabella's social behavior is a bit less divorced from social and moral reality than her brother's—but not much. Like John, Isabella invents her own rules of propriety (both major and minor) to suit the needs of the moment. When James Morland, for example, asks her to dance twice at the same ball, Isabella comments to Catherine: " 'Only conceive, my dear Catherine, what your brother wants me to do. He wants me to dance with him again, though I tell him that it is a most improper thing, and entirely against the rules. It would make us the talk of the place' " (p. 57). To this James replies, somewhat perplexed, " 'Upon my honour . . . in these public assemblies it is as often done as not,' " and the reader can entertain no doubt that he is quite correct (p. 57). Not only does Isabella invent her own rules as she goes along, but in addition, she interprets the significance of other people's social behavior—which is, of course, the outward manifestation of their inward feelings and judgments—in a totally idiosyncratic fashion. The significance which Isabella reads into other people's manners bears virtually no resemblance to the significance those manners would have if interpreted according to the clues contained in the conventional code of propriety. Thus, when Isabella sees a young man, with whom she and Catherine are unacquainted, looking at Catherine, her immediate conclusion is, " 'I am sure he is in love with you' " (p. 41). And when she is informed that the Tilneys seemed out of spirits the day Catherine dined with them, Isabella reads their behavior as symptomatic of "pride, pride, insufferable haughtiness and pride" (p. 129).

To some extent, Isabella's idiosyncratic code of propriety is of an ad hoc nature. She is willing to make up a rule to suit a particular occasion, use it once, and drop it forever. Nonetheless, her code of propriety at all times displays certain characteristic qualities. Isabella's own rules of propriety and mode of interpreting the social behavior of others are drawn from sentimental fiction and disregard, as we have said, the conventional propriety of real life. Like the heroine of a sentimental novel who finds herself drawn by an irresistible affinity towards a mind of similar excellence, Isabella forms friendships which "passed so rapidly through every gradation of increasing tenderness, that there was shortly no fresh proof of it to be given" (p. 37). This "literary" mode of forming friendships ignores the cautious rules of conventional propriety, the purpose of which is, in part, to make it impossible for two people to achieve a high degree of intimacy before they have had time to gain real knowledge of each other's characters. Similarly, in seeing evidences of romantic passion in a passing glance, Isabella is judging manners by the significance they would have in a sentimental novel and disregarding the fact that manners have a very different sort of significance in common life.

Isabella's motives for attempting to import the manners of literature into real life are not difficult to discover. She is a beautiful, but undowered, young woman whose every hope of achieving status, comfort, and respect in life depends on her ability to make a good marriage. Marriage and the flirtation and romance which lead up to it are the only things that have any real significance or interest for Isabella. And the conventions of behavior characterizing the sentimental novel, conventions which attribute extraordinary emotional importance to the most ordinary social behavior, permit Isabella to find the romance she is searching for, virtually everywhere she looks. If she operated according to the minor conventions of everyday propriety, it would be much more difficult for Isabella to think of romance all the time.

The pursuit of a husband for a young lady of Jane Austen's era was necessarily a passive one, mostly a question of waiting to be chosen. Isabella, it is true, makes this pursuit as active as she can, physically chasing good-looking young men through the streets of Bath. Yet it is clear that even though Isabella is willing to violate the major rules of propriety which forbid her to seek a husband actively, the scope for action that will not obviously defeat its own ends is very narrow in this area. Isabella is therefore terribly bored and part of her attempt to live according to the conventions of literature is motivated by her desire to give some interest and significance to her own trammelled existence.[3] By describing her own life as if she were the heroine of a sentimental novel, Isabella can convince herself that she is a fascinating woman experiencing exciting adventures. Thus, she discusses her extremely placid and commonplace romance with James Morland in completely inappropriate terms: " 'The very first moment I beheld him—my heart was irrecoverably gone. . . . Oh! Catherine, the many sleepless nights I have had on your brother's account—. . . I am grown wretchedly thin I know . . .' " (p. 118) etc., etc.

All this reflects not only Isabella's boredom and her anxiety about her own fate, but also her vanity and her overweaning desire for attention and consequence. She wishes to seem fascinating not only in her own eyes, but also in the eyes of others. Jane Austen does not overlook any of the pressures which make Isabella's behavior what it is, yet she has no sympathy with her. One of the most fundamental points made in *Northanger Abbey* is simply that decent and intelligent people must come to terms with the fact that real life is usually dull, that it provides only restricted opportunities for action, and that most people (even if they are well above average in every way) can hope neither to be exciting in themselves, nor born to exciting fates. Early in the novel, Jane Austen describes a conversation between Catherine and Miss Tilney in which "not an observation was made, nor an expression used by either which had not been made and used some thousands of times before . . . in every Bath season" (p. 72). But Jane Austen does not censure Catherine and Miss Tilney for the fact that their remarks are totally unoriginal in content. Instead, she congratulates them on the manner in which they have spoken: "with simplicity and truth and without personal conceit" (p. 72). For this is, indeed, "something uncommon" (p. 72). Catherine and Miss Tilney are to be congratulated because boredom and conceit are not strong enough forces in their natures—as they are in Isabella's—to make them wish to escape from the restrictions of dull reality. They have come to terms with their own essential ordinariness. It is, of course, ironic that true adventure will come to both of them—as it never will to Isabella —yet they would not be rational if they were to expect it, and they would be less rational still if they were to expect it as a part of every day's program. The minor rules of propriety receive Jane Austen's approval in *Northanger Abbey* because she believes them to be based upon an understanding and an acceptance of the restrictive realities of everyday life. The proprieties of the sentimental novel, according to which Isabella attempts to live, however, are based upon an attempt to transcend the restrictions of everyday reality and to achieve a freer and more exciting state of being. Such an attempt Jane Austen believes to be doomed from the start, simply because most human beings, and therefore their everyday lives, are extremely limited.

And Isabella's is not the only example of an attempt to import the conventions of literature into real life which can be found in *Northanger Abbey*. Indeed the novel is full of attacks on a variety of false and unrealistic conventions of taste, emotion, language, and manners, ultimately drawn from the world of the sentimental novel, which have become acceptable in polite society. The convention of taste which dictates that everyone must get tired of Bath after six weeks, for example, is derived from the common assumption of sentimental fiction that truly exalted minds are peculiarly susceptible to the charms of nature. Yet the very people who profess a disgust with Bath and a passion for the country, as Henry Tilney points out, " 'lengthen their six weeks into ten or twelve, and go away at last because they can afford to stay no longer'" (p. 28). Similarly, the manners of the fop, which Henry parodies, derive from fiction their basic assumption that the most trivial relationships between a man and a woman must be charged with emotion. Thus, when Catherine tells Henry that she has been in Bath about a week, he replies:

> "Really!" with affected astonishment.
> "Why should you be surprized, sir?"
> "Why, indeed!" said he, in his natural tone—"but some emotion must appear to be raised by your reply" (p. 26).

All these basically literary conventions of taste and proprieties of behavior have gained currency because people wish to give to their own daily lives some of the excitement characteristic of the lives of fictional heroes. But Jane Austen points out that no set of proprieties can make sense unless it accepts, as its starting point, the fact that real life—not invariably, as Catherine will discover, but basically nonetheless—does not share the excitement of fiction. Real life can be exciting, but it is certainly not exciting all day and every day, and the minor rules of propriety are meant to apply to everyday conduct. When excitement does come into real life, it comes, as we shall see, in its own characteristic manner, which is not the manner of sentimental or gothic fiction.

Since before meeting the Thorpes, Catherine has had virtually no experience with the sort of person who pretends to be something that he is not and who therefore cannot be taken at face value, for a long time it simply does not occur to her to doubt that the Thorpes are exactly the sort of people they pretend to be. John, of course, does not take Catherine in nearly as long as Isabella does. This is partly because his lies and distortions of fact are so blatant and frequent that even the credulous Catherine cannot help noticing them. But Catherine comes to dislike John Thorpe less because she sees through his pretensions than because she dislikes the sort of person he is pretending to be. The role John chooses to play is that of the hard-drinking, free-spending, yet financially shrewd, man-of-the-world, who despises sentiment, ceremony, and literature, who can dominate any social situation, and who never denies himself a pleasure. Catherine never even realizes consciously that John is any thing but the shrewd, skilled, and dominating manipulator of others he believes himself to be—she dislikes him because the sort of man he pretends to be is totally offensive to her both from a moral and from an aesthetic point of view.

With Isabella the case is far different. Isabella presents herself as the heroine of a sentimental novel: full of warm, generous, uncontrollable feelings, loyal to her friends, uninterested in money.[4] Catherine wholeheartedly approves of such a heroine. When Isabella professes a sentiment like, " 'were I mistress of the whole world, your brother would be my only choice' " (p. 119), Catherine finds it a "grand idea" (p. 119). Since Catherine approves of the sort of heroine Isabella is pretending to be, she cannot reject Isabella until she sees through the falseness of Isabella's pretensions. This sort of looking below the surface is something Catherine finds very difficult to do—consciously at least—yet Catherine begins to suspect Isabella before she leaves Bath to visit Northanger Abbey.

While she remains at Bath, Catherine begins to understand Isabella's essential dishonesty only because Isabella's selfishness and vanity often cause her behavior to be radically at variance with the dictates of conventional propriety. And to the rules of conventional propriety, it soon becomes clear, Catherine has a deep and fairly well-considered commitment. When, for example, Mr. Allen hints to Catherine that there may be some impropriety in the unchaperoned drives she has been taking with John Thorpe, Catherine immediately reproaches Mrs. Allen, " 'Dear Madam . . . then why did not you tell me so before? I am sure if I had known it to be improper, I would not have gone with Mr. Thorpe at all' " (p. 104). Considerations of propriety always come before considerations of mere pleasure with Catherine, and not merely because Catherine is afraid to judge and act for herself. Fairly early in the novel, John and Isabella try to convince Catherine to break an engagement she has made to take a country walk with the Tilneys, on the false excuse that she has just been reminded of a prior engagement to drive with them. Catherine's reactions to this incident prove that she has a basically sound, though not a consciously worked-out or really theoretical, understanding of the functions fulfilled by the conventional rules of propriety in an ordered society. In refusing to violate the minor rule of propriety which forbids one to break an engagement merely because one has received a second invitation, Catherine tells the Thorpes, " 'Indeed I cannot go. If I am wrong, I am doing what I believe to be right' " (p. 100). Thinking the incident over later, she reflects that "she had not been withstanding them on selfish principles alone [she does, of course, prefer to go with the Tilneys], she had not consulted merely her own gratification; . . . no, she had attended to what was due to others, and to her own character in their opinion" (p. 101). Catherine understands the basic moral function of the minor rules of propriety: that they provide a fairly sensible guide to the consideration and attention we owe to other people in society. And she also understands that since these rules are commonly accepted and commonly believed to be sensible and moral, we can violate them only at the risk of losing the good opinion of others. Therefore, when Catherine sees Isabella disregarding some of the most significant and moral minor rules of propriety, she begins, though tentatively, to suspect that her friend is not quite the generous and sensitive person she pretends to be. When Isabella urges Catherine to lie to the Tilneys, Catherine is even capable of suspecting that Isabella may in fact be "ungenerous and selfish, regardless of everything but her own gratification" (p. 98). When Isabella's literary pretensions conflict even with the everyday minor rules of propriety, there is never any question that Catherine's approval and allegiance remain with the rules.

Catherine's commitment to both the major and minor rules of conventional propriety is deep. Yet for such an unreflective and unsophisticated young lady, she seems to have a very reliable instinct concerning which minor rules of propriety are important because they have moral significance and which may be safely disregarded, on occasion, because they are matters of custom and ceremony only. A distinction virtually identical to the one made in *Pride and Prejudice* is at issue here. The rules of propriety are divided into those with a basic moral justification (this class includes all the major and many minor rules) and those which are matters of fashion and convenience alone (only minor rules fall into this class). But Catherine's understanding of the distinction, unlike Elizabeth Bennet's, seems to be instinctual, rather than conscious. Catherine is adamant in her refusal to break her engagement with the Tilneys (which would be inconsiderate and hurtful, hence immoral). But after she discovers that John Thorpe has broken the engagement behind her back, she chases the Tilneys home to their lodgings "and the servant still remaining at the open door [which they have just entered], she used only the ceremony of saying that she must speak with Miss Tilney that moment and hurrying by him proceeded upstairs" to set matters right (p. 102). That her mode of entry is highly improper (the general finds it very odd) does not bother Catherine. She seems to sense that on this one occasion she has a rational and moral reason for breaking the minor rule which says that a visitor must wait to be shown in by a servant —and she is quite right in her assumption that the Tilneys will understand and approve her motives. Catherine believes that when an essentially moral or justifiable intention conflicts with a minor rule of propriety, the rule must go. However, her deep commitment to all the rules of conventional propriety simply because they are rules indicates that she does not consider this likely to happen very frequently.

It is difficult, then, for Catherine to appreciate the value of Henry Tilney's somewhat unorthodox manners. His disregard of ceremony, particularly in the interests of a joke, is often striking. Compared to Catherine herself, Henry plays fast and loose with the minor rules of decorum. Catherine sees that Henry's "manner might sometimes surprize" a person deeply committed to the conventional rules of propriety (p. 114). When she first meets him, this leads her to suspect that "he indulged himself a little too much with the foibles of others" (p. 29), in other words, that his unorthodox manners indicated a want of respect for and kindness towards other people. But when she gets to know him better (and, incidentally, falls in love with him) she is able to see, and quite correctly so, that in spite of his frequent disregard of ceremony "his meaning must always be just" (p. 114). The fact that the narrator pokes fun at Catherine's infatuated willingness to admire even "what she did not understand" in Henry's social behavior (p. 114), does not in any way invalidate Catherine's essentially sound estimate of Henry's manners. After Henry reproaches Catherine for the liberties she has been taking with his father's character, she is overwhelmed with guilt and self-reproach and fears she has lost his good opinion forever. But when the two next meet, Henry alters his manners and pays Catherine "rather more attention than usual" (p. 199). This "soothing politeness" gradually raises her spirits "to a modest tranquility" (p. 199). It also proves that Henry understands that the essence of good manners is a generous, moral consideration for others, rather than a lifeless adherence to all the conventional rules of propriety. At the end of the novel, Henry refuses to break, at his Father's command, his tacit engagement to marry Catherine—an incident which parallels Catherine's earlier refusal to break her engagement to walk with Henry and his sister. Like Catherine, Henry will not break the important, moral rules of propriety, but he sets considerably less store than she does on the minor rules which regulate only custom and ceremony. The main difference between Catherine and Henry's views of propriety is that Henry is quite conscious that he violates the conventional minor rules when he feels himself justified in doing so, while Catherine, though she occasionally acts upon this principle, never consciously realizes that technical impropriety is frequently justified.

Catherine's encounters with the Thorpes and with Henry Tilney have demonstrated that though her judgment of others may not be shrewd or penetrating, her instinctive understanding of the nature and function of good manners is basically sound. It is Catherine's encounter with General Tilney—by far the most evil person she meets in the course of the novel—that will reveal the inadequacies of her ideas concerning propriety as tools for understanding others. General Tilney, to an even greater degree than John and Isabella Thorpe, is selfish, vain, pretentious, and ambitious. His manners express his character just as clearly as their manners express theirs. But, unlike John and Isabella, the general is intensely aware of the rules of conventional propriety and though his every action violates the spirit of those rules, their letter is sacred to him. The general's particular pretension is that of good breeding. He describes and considers himself as the most courteous man in the world. When Catherine is first introduced to General Tilney, he receives her with "ready . . . solicitous politeness. . . . To such anxious attention was the General's civility carried that, not aware of her extraordinary swiftness in entering the house [as described above, Catherine has pushed her way past the servant] he was quite angry with the servant whose neglect had reduced her to open the door of the apartment herself . . . it seemed likely that William would lose the favor of his master forever, if not his place, by her rapidity" (p. 102–3). Thus, on General Tilney's first appearance in the story, the character of his manners is clearly revealed. All the ceremonies of civility are offered to Catherine, whom the general wishes to please for purely selfish reasons. All the content of truly proper social behavior is ignored in the general's suspicious and resentful conduct to his blameless, but also helpless, servant.

Catherine, as we have seen, has a deep commitment to the conventional rules of propriety, though she is also willing to dispense with some of their purely ceremonious manifestations. And she is unusually slow in seeing through the pretensions of others. The general's pretension to good breeding, supported as it is by a consistent, if superficial, adherence to the conventional propriety Catherine values, takes Catherine in completely. Insofar as Catherine is able to see through Isabella's pretensions, it is because Isabella's behavior repeatedly and fairly openly violates rules which Catherine understands and approves. But the general pretentiously parades his allegiance to those very rules and for a long time this confuses Catherine deeply. When she dines with the Tilneys, Catherine is puzzled that "in spite of [General Tilney's] great civilities to her—in spite of his thanks, invitations, and compliments —it had been a release to get away from him" (p. 129). When Catherine sees that the forms of conventional propriety are absent from Isabella's behavior, she is capable, though dimly, of suspecting that the moral and emotional content of true propriety is absent too. But with the general, Catherine mistakes the form for the content and fails to realize that the presence of the former is no guarantee of the latter. Catherine's own behavior demonstrates that, tacitly at least, she is able to discriminate between the important or moral and the trivial or merely ceremonial rules of propriety. But that virtually all the major and minor rules can be divorced from their moral content,[5] manipulated in a manner directly contrary to their basic intention, and yet not quite openly violated, simply does not occur to her. Yet this is precisely what General Tilney characteristically does.

> "Well, Eleanor, may I congratulate you on being successful in your application to your fair friend [to visit Northanger]?" [he asks his daughter.]
> "I was just beginning to make the request, sir, as you came in."
> "Well, proceed by all means. I knew how much your heart is in it. My daughter, Miss Morland," he continued, without leaving his daughter time to speak, "has been forming a very bold wish." (p. 139).

Passages such as this one demonstrate that General Tilney's commitment to the proprieties is extremely superficial. Though he pays lip service to the rule of decorum which says he must allow his daughter time to finish the private conversation which he has unwittingly interrupted, in actuality he doesn't let her say another word. The hypocrisy with which he manipulates the forms of politeness is so transparent that Catherine's persistence in viewing him

as a model of decorum becomes striking evidence of an almost patho-
logical inability to look below the surface of social pretence. Before
her visit to Northanger Abbey, Catherine senses something odd
about the general, but is quite unable to define what is wrong. Although one purpose of good manners is to put others at their ease,
the general's behavior makes Catherine intensely uncomfortable.
However, she attributes this discomfort solely to "her own stupidity" and not to something lacking in his manners (p. 129).

When she is thrown into intimate contact with General Tilney, as
a guest in his house, prolonged and close observation of his character forces Catherine to consider the question of why "so charming a man seemed always a check upon his children's spirits" (p.
156), why everyone is afraid of him in spite of his ostentatious politeness. It is in attempting to solve this mystery—and for her it really
is a mystery—that Catherine first tries to apply the notions she has
recently derived from gothic fiction to real life. It is not unnatural
that General Tilney should remind Catherine of a gothic villain.
The unmitigated evil that she senses in him is, as we shall see,
really there. What gothic fiction has taught Catherine is that evil
men, such as she suspects the general of being, express their wicked-
ness in violent ways, but shroud their crimes in the deepest mystery.
Two ways of solving the puzzle of the general are open to Catherine. The correct way is to conclude that General Tilney's superficially civil manners are not good manners, because they actually
express his selfishness and egotism in a disguised, but perfectly
recognisable, form. The incorrect, "gothic" way—which Catherine,
characteristically, adopts—is to accept his conventionally proper
manners at face value (as good manners, that is) and to conclude
that those manners are an elaborate blind which conceals his real,
horrible character. Thus, Catherine's first conclusion about the general is that there is a radical disparity between his good manners and
his bad morals, and that those bad morals have expressed themselves
*only* in secret crime. Such a conclusion is supported both by the
view of human nature Catherine has found in the gothic novels she
read at Bath and by her own unquestioned value for the forms of
conventional propriety as good in themselves.

Henry and Eleanor Tilney, it might be added, are not in the
least confused about their father's character or manner, and both
attempt to enlighten Catherine on these points by discreet hints.
But the rules of propriety demanding filial respect prohibit Henry
and Eleanor from speaking openly about General Tilney's faults

and Catherine, for a long while, consistently misinterprets their hints in accordance with her gothic preconceptions. Eleanor's decorous attempts to enlighten Catherine about the general invariably misfire. On Catherine's first morning at Northanger, for example, the general wishes to take an early walk at the precise moment when Catherine fervently wants to be shown around the Abbey. Characteristically, he masks his selfishness beneath the forms of propriety. " 'Which would she [Catherine] prefer? He was equally at her service.—Which did his daughter think would most accord with her fair friend's wishes?—But . . . Yes, he certainly read in Miss Morland's eyes a judicious desire of making use of the present smiling weather.—. . . He yielded implicitly and would fetch his hat' " (p. 177). No less characteristically, Catherine accepts his speech at face value and laments to Eleanor "that he should be taking them out of doors against his own inclination, under a mistaken idea of pleasing her" (p. 177). Eleanor, who is well aware of her father's motives and meaning, is confused by the fact that propriety forbids her to speak openly and says only, " 'Do not be uneasy on my father's account, he always walks out at this time of day' " (p. 177). This hint seems plain enough, but Catherine "did not exactly know how [it] was to be understood. Why was Miss Tilney embarrassed? Could there be any unwillingness on the General's side to show her over the Abbey?" (p. 177). And it is at this moment that the idea of a dark crime which General Tilney has committed within the Abbey's walls begins to take form in Catherine's mind. If Catherine had been able to understand the general's manners on her own or from Eleanor and Henry's hints, her gothic delusions would have had no mystery to give them their start.

Henry's hints about his father—never as guarded as Eleanor's—grow gradually more open as he comes to know Catherine better. It is mostly as a result of Henry's instruction that Catherine finally comes to a valid understanding of the general's character and manners—and we must next examine the process by which she reaches this understanding. To a large degree, Henry's own manners can be seen as a reaction against his father's social behavior. The general respects the forms of propriety while disregarding their spirit. Henry, on the other hand, tends to be rather careless about the minor forms, but is at all times considerate of others and faithful in discharging his moral obligations. Henry can refer to Eleanor in public, most improperly, as "my stupid sister" (p. 113), yet his company and kindness are clearly her greatest comforts. General Tilney, on the other hand, is scrupulously polite to his daughter, yet tries her patience continually and severely. Henry's own manners provide a running commentary on those of his father and it is her observation of Henry, as we have noted, that first suggests to Catherine that "meaning" may sometimes be more significant than "manner." Thus Henry's manners have provided Catherine, from the beginning, with the key to General Tilney's mystery. But Henry's explicit instructions are also needed if Catherine is to learn how to use that key.

Puzzled by the disparity she finds between the general's "good" manners and the evil which she senses is a part of his character, Catherine, as we have seen, invents a gothic solution.[6] The general is a criminal, probably a wife-murderer, who carefully hides his true character under a mask of propriety. Luckily for Catherine, Henry discovers her suspicions (which are not very well concealed) and reads her a long lecture on their injustice. " 'Dear Miss Morland, consider the dreadful nature of the suspicions you have entertained. What have you been judging from? Remember the country and the age in which we live. . . . Consult your own understanding, your own sense of the probable, your own observation of what is passing around you.—Does our education prepare us for such atrocities? Do our laws connive at them? Could they be perpetrated without being known, in a country like this, where social and literary intercourse is on such a footing; where every man is surrounded by a neighborhood of voluntary spies, and where roads and newspapers lay everything open?" (pp. 197–8). This is an interesting speech. In the first place, Henry makes no real attempt to defend his father's character; he does not claim that his father is a good man who would not wish to commit a murder under any circumstances. No, Henry's defense of his father from Catherine's charges rests on quite other premises. The basic assumption here is that even criminals are rational and are not likely to commit crimes that are going to be discovered and punished. And the age is such a public and suspicious one that a prominent man like the general could not hope to murder his wife and escape exposure and ruin. Therefore, the general probably did not murder his wife. This, it seems to me, is the logical structure of the argument Henry is making here. Evil exists, as Catherine now suspects, but evil people are not going to act in ways that will get them into trouble. For they can easily find ways of expressing their true natures without openly violating the accepted "laws of the land, and the manners of the age" (p. 200). This, of course, is what General Tilney does.[7]

Henry's lecture makes a deep impression on Catherine, but she does not really understand it. In the first place, she is somewhat confused by Henry's assertion that his father loved his mother as well as such a cold man can love anyone. In making this claim, Henry is not trying to prove to Catherine that his father is basically a good man. On the contrary, he refers explicitly to his father's bad temper and lack of tenderness and says nothing that indicates a belief that the general might not have had criminal impulses of various sorts toward people other than his wife. But this distinction is lost upon Catherine. She now sees that "the manners of the age" must be "some security for the existence even of a wife not beloved" (p. 200), but she again makes her characteristic error of confounding "manner" and "meaning," or "habit" and "heart." If the manners of the age do not permit murder, if the general has not, in fact, murdered his wife, then Catherine concludes that the impulse to commit murder or other sorts of crime must also be absent from the general's psychological makeup. Yet this is precisely the assertion that Henry Cleverly avoids making. "Among the Alps and Pyrenees [where the extreme manners of gothic fiction hold sway]," Catherine muses, "perhaps there were no mixed characters. There, such as were not spotless as an angel, might have the dispositions of a fiend. But . . . among the English, she believed, in their *hearts and habits,* there was a general, though unequal, mixture of good and bad" (p. 200, my italics). Because English laws and manners forbid murder or other extreme forms of violence, Catherine concludes that there are no English fiends. And since the general has been cleared from her "grossly injurious suspicions" (p. 200), the most Catherine is willing to say against him is that he is "not perfectly amiable" (p. 200). Though the narrator presents Catherine's conclusions without apparent irony of tone, it soon becomes clear that Catherine is mistaken in her belief that General Tilney's is a mixed character containing more good than bad.

Henry soon becomes aware that in spite of his instructions, the removal of her gothic delusion has left Catherine with the almost equally erroneous belief that the general's superficially civil manners are evidence of a basically sound, if not perfectly amiable, character. When the general civilly remarks that Henry need pay no special attention to the dinner he is to give for his family at

Woodston, Catherine as usual accepts the statement at face value. Henry is forced to tell her quite openly that the general is being insincere and, in fact, expects a superb dinner to be prepared for him. This is a revelation to Catherine. "The inexplicability of the General's conduct dwelt much on her thoughts . . . why he should say one thing so positively, and mean another all the while, was most unaccountable! How were people, at that rate, to be understood?" (p. 211). Catherine has finally asked herself the appropriate question. How can people be understood if the forms of good manners are no guarantee that the content is present? The answer is breathtakingly simple: people's pretensions to good manners must be consciously and continually questioned, not only when, as with Isabella and John Thorpe, the forms are often absent, but also, as with General Tilney, when the forms appear to be present.

The revelation of Isabella's two-faced conduct toward Catherine's brother James provides a catalyst which arranges all Catherine's earlier vague suspicions of her friend in a clear and ordered pattern. She realizes at last that Isabella " 'is a vain coquette . . . she never had any regard either for James or for me' " (p. 218). Similarly, General Tilney's character must be revealed in a dramatic and unmistakeable form if Catherine is to understand it—and fortunately for Catherine, such a revelation is made. General Tilney has been courting Catherine as a wife for Henry under the mistaken impression that she is an heiress on a spectacular scale. Learning his mistake, he turns her from his house in the rudest possible manner and orders his son to think of her no more. Henry, however, is delightfully loyal to Catherine and when he tells her the whole story of his father's motives, Catherine concludes "that in suspecting General Tilney of either murdering or shutting up his wife, she had scarcely sinned against his character or magnified his cruelty" (p. 247). This is Catherine's final judgment of the general and I believe it to be essentially valid, in spite of the fact that it sounds less balanced than her earlier conclusion that the general had a mixed character.

Jane Austen seems to have in mind here a simple estimate of the moral significance of murder which she considers relevant to General Tilney's behavior. Murder may be conceived as a totally egotistical act. For in practical terms, even if he is not aware of it, a murderer necessarily values his own desires or needs at an infinitely higher rate than those of his victim. Even the victim's right to live cannot influence the murderer, who must think only of himself.

Now this sort of unbounded selfishness, which I think Jane Austen has in mind here as part of the very definition of a murderer, is the general's most prominent character trait. And when General Tilney expells Catherine from his house, Jane Austen means us to see his action as a domestic parody of a killing. Catherine's continued existence in the general's vicinity has become highly disagreeable to him and in this respect Catherine resembles the typical murder victim. The general, like a real murderer, wants his victim eliminated as completely and quickly as possible from his world. In turning Catherine out of his house without the slightest consideration for the rights which the code of propriety gives her at his hands, the general parodies the actions of the murderer whose own interests necessarily are more important to him than any of his victim's rights. As Catherine now realizes, the general really is something of a fiend.

The difference between General Tilney and the average gothic villain, then, is not to be found in the quantity or quality of evil in their hearts. Rather it resides, as Henry has known all along, in the manner in which that evil is expressed. Murder is quite decorous in gothic fiction, but in England it is likely to be punished, for it violates the laws and manners of the age. Villians like General Tilney will therefore tend to express their evil impulses without defying law and custom openly enough to get themselves into trouble. General Tilney, of course, represents an extreme manifestation of this tendency. His manners invariably express the evil in his heart, but General Tilney is able to preserve all the forms of conventional propriety intact, except on the one occasion when he expells Catherine from Northanger. Here, his wrath and resentment are so great that they simply cannot be expressed within even the purely formal constraints of his usual code of propriety. However, it is significant that even in his most extreme wrath, the general violates only the minor rules of propriety and not the laws of the realm. At the worst, he has exposed himself to such halfhearted censure as Mrs. Allen's, " 'I really have not patience with the General' " (p. 238)—but he is certainly safe from any serious form of punishment. And this, it seems to me, is what Catherine must learn about the difference between life and gothic fiction: the same evil and potential for violence are present in both, but in real life evil tends to be expressed in ways which are customary and socially acceptable and which therefore expose the evil doer to little risk of punishment. And the rules of propriety, though basically moral in intention, in practice are quite flexible enough to permit bad people to express the evil in their hearts without getting themselves into serious trouble. Life and fiction differ in "manner" more than in "meaning." It is only by realizing how completely a conventionally proper manner can be divorced from the basic moral meaning it ought to have, that Catherine can come to understand the relationship between General Tilney and the typical gothic villain.

Catherine's original gothic fantasies about General Tilney represent a garbling of the truth, rather than a complete delusion. And when she reacts to Henry's remonstrance by concluding that there is no resemblance between life and gothic fiction and that the general is a mixed character whose professions of civility and generosity have at least some value, Catherine is as far from the truth as ever. It is only at the end of the novel (and with the help of a very complete revelation), that Catherine begins to gain some real understanding of General Tilney. The narrator describes General Tilney's letter consenting to Henry and Catherine's marriage as a document "very courteously worded in a page full of empty professions" (p. 252). I think we can assume that the narrator's viewpoint here is now shared by Catherine. Catherine has finally realized that courteous professions can be empty, that the forms of good manners are ultimately quite separable from the inward virtues they are supposed to represent. Catherine has never, as we have seen, made this mistake in her conduct—her manners have always been based on good morals and a realistic, if tacit, understanding of what is important in social behavior. But she has been only too willing to accept other people's unsupported pretensions to good manners or good taste at their own valuations. Catherine's rejection of Isabella Thorpe and General Tilney shows that she finally realizes that in her own era a more or less well-supported pretension to virtue and propriety is the characteristic manner of evil.

# STATUS,
# WORK, AND
# PROPRIETY IN
# *MANSFIELD PARK*

*Mansfield Park* is at present Jane Austen's most unpopular novel. Two aspects of it, especially, have tended to annoy readers and puzzle critics: the episode of the amateur theatricals and the question of Fanny's moral judgment. Why, readers have wondered, should Jane Austen condemn the innocent amusement of play-acting so severely in this novel? Why should theatricals be almost a crime at Mansfield Park when they were a favorite amusement in the Austens' own home at Steventon? In addition, many of the novel's readers have been uncertain what to make of Fanny's character. Sickly, timid, humorless, sometimes self-righteous, often very severe in her moral judgments of others, Fanny is generally felt to be a highly unattractive character, yet she seems to receive a greater share of Jane Austen's moral approval than any other character in the novel.[1] How is one to resolve the apparent disparity between Fanny's status as a personality and her status as a moral agent?

As a whole, *Mansfield Park* contains fewer characters who can be described as moral nonentities—that is, characters, who exist on such a low plane of complexity, awareness, or intelligence that it becomes absurd to think of them as making conscious moral choices for good or evil—than any of Jane Austen's other novels.[2] And when the characters in *Mansfield Park* are considered as moral agents, it is apparent that they fall into two clearly marked categories: those possessing a fairly well-defined set of moral principles according to which they attempt, though with varying degress of success, to judge and act, and those who, lacking any appreciable degree of "principle, active principle" (p. 463), are forced, almost entirely, to follow the dictates of feeling and worldly wisdom as guides to moral choice. These categories are quite discrete and it should always be clear to the reader in which one a particular character belongs,[3] but as categories they are not confining or simplistic. A character may attempt, fairly consistently, to judge and act according to moral principles of the highest order, but for several reasons this attempt does not assure success in making sound moral judgments. The principles themselves, though endorsed in good faith, may be mistaken, or the agent's feelings may unconsciously bias his moral decisions or his practical estimates of the motives and personalities involved in actual moral decisions may be naive or unintelligent, though his principles are sound. Hence, characters in *Mansfield Park* belonging to the category of principled moral agents are not in any sense meant to be accepted as models of moral infallibility. Likewise, the characters without principles, who judge primarily according to their own desires and feelings as individuals, are not necessarily going to be wrong in all their moral decisions. Feelings may, fortuitously, lead one to make the very moral choice which sound principle, rigorously applied, would dictate and worldly wisdom may prompt a type of caution which superficially resembles principled behavior.

But though these two categories will not provide a simple guide to the moral status of the characters in *Mansfield Park,* they are nonetheless highly significant, for if we examine the causes which produce a character of either the principled or the nonprincipled sort, we will come to grips with one of the basic moral values of the novel and will, incidentally, cast some light on the book's two most perplexing aspects: the play and the character of Fanny. What part the rules of propriety play in the life of an individual in *Mansfield Park* is almost completely dependent upon whether that individual does or does not see decorous behavior as one of the outward or social manifestations of an inward commitment to moral principle.

It is a fairly simple and unambiguous task to determine whether a character in *Mansfield Park* is trying to live according to principle or not—though it is a more difficult matter to determine whether he is indeed succeeding. Fanny, obviously, is making the attempt. She struggles throughout the novel to do her duty by the family at Mansfield Park, which has, in its quite limited way, been kind to her. Her character, in this respect, is clear to all, and even Henry Crawford feels a love for her which, the narrator remarks, "was inspired by the knowledge of her being well-principled and religious" (p. 294). Edmund also lives a life in which principle is an important force. Before he can decide to propose to Mary Crawford he must convince himself—even if erroneously—that her morals are basically sound and when his sister Maria elopes with Henry Crawford, Fanny immediately feels that the blow will be doubly strong to one of Edmund's "upright principles" (p. 442). William Price, too, has only to be given an opportunity to speak upon the subject of his beloved profession, the navy, to give Sir Thomas "the proof of [his] good principles," and to make Henry Crawford feel "the glory of heroism, of usefulness, of exertion, of endurance" (p. 236). Sir Thomas, too, is obviously a man of "principle as well as pride," and he has "a general wish of doing right" (p. 4), upon which he tries to base his actions. Unfortunately, his principles are, as we shall see, not as sound as Fanny's, Edmund's, or William's, and he is, furthermore, less honest and consistent in his application of those principles than they are, throughout most of the novel. But though he is far from being presented as a moral ideal, Sir Thomas is definitely a man trying to live up to a moral code and obviously belongs in the category of principled characters. A few minor characters complete this category: Mrs. Grant, whose behavior to her difficult husband shows she has an ideal of wifely duty, and Susan Price who "brought up in the midst of negligence and error" has nonetheless "formed . . . proper opinions of what ought to be" (pp. 397–8).[4]

The category of nonprincipled characters is much larger, comprising as it does all the remaining men and women in the novel, except Lady Bertram who alone seems morally a cipher. Fanny feels quite accurately, that Henry Crawford possesses "no principle to supply as a duty what the heart was deficient in" (p. 329). Edmund is correct when he says of Mary Crawford, "her's are faults of principle" (p. 456), and Sir Thomas puts his finger on the main defect in the education he has given his daughters when he concludes that "principle, active principle, had been wanting" (p. 463). Tom Bertram, until his conversion at the end of the novel, is characterized by "thoughtlessness and selfishness" (p. 462), while Mrs. Norris is a hypocrite on both the conscious and the unconscious levels, describing and considering herself as prudent, self-denying, and useful to others, but actually consulting only the inclinations of her own miserly, restless, and interfering temperament in all her doings. The nonprincipled minor characters, onstage and off—Mr. Rushworth, his mother, the elder Prices, Mr. Yates, Admiral and Mrs. Crawford,

Lady Stornaway, and Mrs. Fraser—are too numerous to be discussed individually, but their status in this regard is clear.

In addition, a character's view of propriety is in *Manfield Park* very closely correlated with the question of principle. In general, the principled characters in the novel tend to see the socially accepted rules of propriety, at their best, as outward manifestations of the moral principles to which they are committed. To these individuals, for example, the respectful behavior toward parents which the rules of propriety dictate is simply the social manifestation of an internal commitment to traditional family structure and to the principle that children owe their parents gratitude and duty for the care they have received.[5] This view of manners, of course, represents a basic social purpose served by both the major and minor rules of propriety: these rules of behavior ought, ideally, to enforce patterns of behavior which are consistent with the moral values of the society. Jane Austen is well aware that the minor rules of propriety are often perverted from this laudable purpose and made to serve the ends of mere fashion or caprice, but the principled characters in *Mansfield Park* try, at their best, to separate "true," or basically moral, rules of propriety from those rules of propriety that have been warped by considerations of fashion—and to live by the former set of rules alone. This ideal of true propriety by which the principled characters in *Mansfield Park* live is quite similar to the ideal of true propriety suggested in *Pride and Prejudice* and *Northanger Abbey*. As in these two novels, so in *Mansfield Park* it is tacitly assumed that the conventional rules of propriety governing behavior in crucially important social situations (i.e., the rule that an engaged woman should not flirt with a man other than her fiancé) are all obviously moral in nature, hence sacrosanct. The validity of this group of rules, which I designated major rules in my discussion of *Sense and Sensibility,* is simply not questioned in *Mansfield Park,* or in *Pride and Prejudice* and *Northanger Abbey*.

The most notable difference between the two standards of propriety is that true propriety in *Mansfield Park* is sanctioned solely by its connection with moral principles, whereas true propriety in *Pride and Prejudice* and *Northanger Abbey* is sanctioned both by its connection with good morals and by its connection with sound common sense. In *Mansfield Park* the stress falls on the individual's obligation to obey the morally valid rules of propriety, whereas in *Pride and Prejudice* the individual's right to disobey minor rules of propriety that are not sensible and functional is also emphasized. Hence the code of propriety by which the principled characters in *Mansfield Park* try to live is more repressive in its nature than Elizabeth Bennet's code—though not radically different in its justification. In *Mansfield Park,* the principled characters place a good deal of stress on the importance of manners, for to them manners and morals are integrally related, two aspects of the same phenomenon and almost equally vital to their views of themselves.

The nonprincipled characters, however, like a good many characters in the earlier novels, tend to ignore the moral aspect of the rules of propriety. To these characters, both the major and minor rules of propriety are an entirely social phenomenon, a set of behavior prescriptions which define one's social position. The fact that these behavior prescriptions are derived—or ought to be derived—from a set of moral principles is not clear to this group of characters. It is elegance, rather than strict propriety of manner, that really matters to them. The Bertram girls, for example, are "distinguished for elegance and accomplishments" (p. 463), and Mary Crawford, too, is elegant in manner, though capable of making an ill-bred remark now and then. To these young women good manners represent part of a conscious claim to high social position and are valued as such. Viewing decorum in this light, the nonprincipled characters in the novel are naturally not as deeply committed to an ideal of good manners as are the principled characters whose decorous behavior is an integral part of their moral ideals.

Early in the novel a series of informal conversations portrays the very different views of propriety held by the principled and nonprincipled characters: the former group sees good manners as the outward manifestation of good principles and an integral part of good moral character, the latter group sees good manners as a purely social accomplishment like playing the harp (Mary Crawford's harp, incidentally, is "as elegant as herself" [p. 65]) and almost equally unconnected with the internal realities of character. The two most important conversations dealing with the nature of propriety and the purpose of good manners take place mainly between Edmund and Mary Crawford. Fanny is the theme of the first conversation and takes a subsidiary part in the second. Mary initiates the first discussion by asking Edmund and Tom, " 'Pray, is [Fanny Price] out or is she not?' " (p. 48). Mary is puzzled because there is a very strict code of behavior in the fashionable world governing the demeanor of girls before and after they have "come out" in society—a code to which Fanny's behavior does not seem to conform. "'A girl not out,'" as Mary explains, "'has always the same sort of dress; a close bonnet for instance, looks very demure and never says a word. . . . Girls should be quiet and modest'" (p. 49). Tom Bertram, who also looks at manners primarily as behavioral claims to a particular social status, understands Mary completely and is easily able to supply examples from his large social circle of the alteration in demeanor that comes over a girl when she comes out. Yet Fanny's behavior, closely examined, corresponds to neither the model for a girl not out, nor to the model for a grown-up young lady. Edmund understands the fashionable standard of propriety to which Mary is appealing, but stoutly denies its applicability to the simpler and presumably more moral world of Mansfield. "'I will not undertake to answer the question [of whether Fanny is out or not],'" he says, "'My cousin is grown up. She has the age and sense of a woman, but the outs and not outs are beyond me'" (p. 49). Edmund is claiming here—correctly—that Fanny's social behavior springs naturally from her age and her intelligence and is an integral part of her character, unlike the social behavior of girls who live by the fashionable, but morally distorted, code of out and not out, a code which demands a radical change in behavior at a point in life when character is altering only slowly.[6] Edmund adds further that these fashionable girls "'are ill brought up. . . . They are always acting upon motives of vanity and there is no more real modesty in their behavior *before* they appear in public, than afterwards'" (p. 50)—because their behavior is merely a social trick, not, like Fanny's, the expression of their internal character. Mary, however, is unable to understand Edmund's point and after asking a few more purely social questions about where Fanny dines and whether she goes to balls is able to say decisively, "'Oh! then the point is clear. Miss Price is *not* out'" (p. 51).

The second discussion of the nature of true propriety takes place immediately after Mary has found out that Edmund intends to become a clergyman. "'A clergyman,'" Mary tells Edmund emphatically, "'is nothing'" (p. 92), and he replies that, "'I cannot call that situation nothing which . . . has the guardianship of religion and morals and consequently of the manners which result from their influence'" (p. 92). Mary again misunderstands the significance of the term manners as Edmund uses it and asks him how the sermons of the clergy can "'fashion the manners'" (the choice of the word "fashion" is surely significant) of a fashionable society "'where [the clergy] are so seldom seen themselves'" (p. 92). Edmund again attempts to explain that by manners he means social behavior springing from moral commitment:

> "A clergyman cannot . . . set the tone in dress . . . a good clergyman will be useful in his parish and his neighborhood, where the parish and neighborhood are of a size capable of knowing his private character, and observing his general conduct, which in London can rarely be the case. . . . And with regard to their influencing public manners, Miss Crawford must not misunderstand me, or suppose I mean to call them the arbiters of good-breeding, the regulators of refinement and courtesy, the master of the ceremonies of life. The *manners* I speak of might rather be called *conduct,* perhaps, the result of good principles; the effect, in short, of those doctrines which it is their duty to teach and recommend" (pp 92–93).

Fanny, of course, agrees "with gentle earnestness" (p. 93), but Mary says only, "'I am as much surprised now as I was at first that you should intend to take orders. You really are fit for something better. Come, do change your mind. . . . Go into the law'" (p. 93).

In these two discussions, Mary (backed in the first by Tom Bertram) indicates that she, and by implication the novel's other non-principled characters as well, is completely unable to see that manners have an important moral dimension. Edmund and Fanny demonstrate not only that they do understand this point, but also that they see Mansfield Park as a place ruled by truer standards of decorum than those of the fashionable world, a place where the outs and not outs are irrelevant and where the manners of the conscientious clergy are more highly respected than the manners of the man about town.

Thus, in *Mansfield Park,* more than in any of the earlier novels, a devastating attack is being made upon the standard of propriety current in fashionable society. In neither *Sense and Sensibility* nor *Pride and Prejudice* does the reader get a sense, as he does in *Mansfield Park,* that the heroine must consciously renounce polite society's corrupt concept of propriety in order to understand the nature of true propriety. In *Pride and Prejudice,* it is Miss Bingley whose behavior (though she herself is unaware of this) deviates from polite society's best standard of decorum, the standard to which Elizabeth and Darcy finally conform. But in *Mansfield Park* it is suggested that polite society as a whole is adopting a corrupt standard of decorum—one which the novel's principled characters must reject. In a very real sense, Edmund and Fanny would cease to be themselves if their manners were fashionably stylish and charming, for manners must at all times express their moral commitment and moral commitment in the Crawfords' London world is unfashionable and inelegant. Further, unlike *Pride and Prejudice* and *Northanger Abbey, Mansfield Park* raises the possibility that the divergence between polite society's corrupt standards of propriety and morally acceptable standards may not merely be confined to the minor rules of propriety governing everyday social interaction, but may extend as well to the major rules regulating both behavior in crucially important social situations and the handling of the most important social and familial relationships. It is not merely on the question of "out" and "not out" that polite society is following a code of role-playing behavior different from the one Edmund and Fanny advocate. In the course of the novel, the behavior of the nonprincipled characters, whose only loyalty is to the fashionable code of propriety, proves that this code has no strict rules governing truly respectful behavior to parents, loyalty to a fiancé, or straightforwardness in matters of courtship (all definitely major aspects of propriety in Jane Austen's view). Ultimately, when Mary Crawford tells Edmund that though his sister Maria has committed adultery with Henry Crawford, if the two marry polite society will accept them, we realize that even the major rules of propriety governing the relationship of a wife with her husband have little importance in polite society's code of decorum.

The validity of the major rules is never seriously questioned in *Mansfield Park*. The novel presents a situation in which characters who violate these major rules by that very action clearly and unmistakably demonstrate their own moral corruption and call down punishment upon themselves. This happens in the cases of Maria, Julia, Henry, Mary, and Tom—all of whom violate major rules of propriety. This situation is very different from that of *Sense and Sensibility*, where Marianne's violation of the major rules governing courtships and engagements demonstrates only that she holds a theory of social behavior at variance with the one embodied in the major rules of propriety. Marianne's disagreement with the premises of the major rules of propriety calls the validity of those premises into question—at least temporarily. Her disobedience to the major rules is not taken, a priori, as incontrovertible evidence of moral failing on her part. However, this is precisely the significance that disobedience to

the major rules does have in *Mansfield Park* and that is why I assert
that the validity of the major rules is not seriously questioned in this
novel.

Fashionable society in *Mansfield Park,* sets little stress on these
srtict major rules, and hence it is seen as very corrupt. The standard
of propriety to which Edmund and Fanny adhere seems to be an
earlier and more rural one—one which has not yet been altered by
recent social developments. Edmund and Fanny's code is definitely
a conventional—in the sense of traditional—one. But unlike Elizabeth Bennet's code, theirs would be seen as an anchronism in the
polite society of contemporary London. Hence, we must realize that
throughout *Mansfield Park* a tension between two full-blown standards of propriety, both conventional in one sense of the term, is at
issue. In this respect, *Mansfield Park* differs from all the other novels
which assume that there is only one basic standard of propriety, with
variations.

In their belief that Mansfield is a bastion of true propriety, as they
define it, however, Edmund and Fanny are at least partially mistaken. Mansfield is indeed the abode of "elegance, propriety, regularity, harmony" (p. 391) and Sir Thomas certainly has a very "high
sense of . . . decorum" (p. 442), but because Sir Thomas's principles
are not completely sound, the decorum of Mansfield does not correspond to the ideal of true propriety. To anticipate somewhat we
may say here that Sir Thomas's basically good principles are warped
by a large infusion of the false wordly values of money and status,
and the decorum of Mansfield, if not quite the totally external
decorum of the Crawfords' circle in London, is still more concerned
with purely social consequence and less with the heart and conscience than it ought to be.[7] Sir Thomas has a great belief in the
dignity of his own position and his manners are too often merely a
means of impressing that dignity on others, too seldom an expression of disinterested strict fairness, strict uprightness, or general
good will. Thus, Sir Thomas gives Fanny the use of his carriage for
her first dinner visit less from consideration of her health or comfort
than from a feeling that it would be discreditable for *"my niece* to
walk to a dinner engagement at this time of year!" (p. 221, my
italics). Sir Thomas is a very formal man, who values his position
in society too highly and at the expense of more important considerations, and his manners are too often merely a matter of social forms.
He has brought up each of his daughters "to practise politeness as
a duty. . . . But the want of that higher species of self-command,

that just consideration of others, that knowledge of her own heart, that principle of right which had not formed an essential part of her education" (p. 91) causes Julia, as well as Maria, to see his formal and strict rules of propriety as annoying restrictions on her freedom of action. The Crawfords' circle in London lives by a standard of propriety that makes no pretence of reflecting an internal moral commitment. The standard of decorum which Sir Thomas imposes at Mansfield upon the reluctant and the willing alike, however, does make this pretence. But unfortunately the hypocrisy which characterizes so many of the inmates of Mansfield, including (as we shall see) Sir Thomas himself, thrives in such a situation. If they behave with strict external propriety, Sir Thomas does not inquire closely into his children's feelings and motives—so the formality of behavior upon which Sir Thomas insists at Mansfield, conceals all sorts of deplorable feelings. By failing to realize that outward propriety may not be a certain sign of inward moral rectitude, Sir Thomas is— at least at first—effectively prevented from looking below the surface to distinguish between Fanny's true propriety and the hypocrisy of Julia or Maria. And since Edmund and Fanny do really have a moral commitment to Sir Thomas's standards of propriety, they fail to see the large element of hypocrisy which motivates much of Mansfield's "elegance, propriety, regularity, harmony" (p. 391). Thus we see that the principled and nonprincipled characters in the novel have radically different views of the nature of decorum and that the flaws in Sir Thomas's own principles and perceptions have prevented Mansfield Park from becoming the bastion of true "old-fashioned" decorum that he, Edmund, and Fanny believe it to be.

There are, I think, two closely related factors which, taken together, are mainly responsible for determining whether a character in *Mansfield Park* does or does not possess a set of active principles.[8] The first and less important of these is the question of status. Among the younger generation, all those who turn out to lack principle—Mary and Henry Crawford, Tom, Maria, and Julia Bertram—possess as a birthright a very high and supremely assured status within their society, a status of which nothing but the grossest misconduct, like Maria's, can possibly deprive them. Mary Crawford has £20,000, Henry Crawford has a very good estate, and both are well-born. Tom Bertram must become a wealthy and influential baronet some day no matter how badly he behaves, and Sir Thomas points out that the "rank, fortune, rights, and expectations" (p. 11) of his daughters will always be immeasurably higher

than those of Fanny Price simply because they *are* his daughters.
On the other hand, the Price children occupy a very low status
indeed. Fanny is considered extremely lucky to be taken on as an
unpaid semiservant and poor relation at Mansfield Park, and the
other young Prices must rely on their own efforts to lift themselves
above the squalid life led by their parents. Edmund's status is rather
ambiguous. As Mary Crawford says, "Sir Thomas Bertram's son is
somebody" (p. 289), but, on the other hand, Edmund has no fortune
and if he is to live at all must fit himself for the relatively humble
position of a clergyman. At any rate, it can be safely said that Edmund is not, like the Crawfords, Tom, Maria, and Julia, born into a
position which is completely satisfactory in terms both of social rank
and of wealth, and which is completely assured regardless (within
very wide limits) of how its possessor chooses to behave. Like the
young Prices, Edmund must to some degree make his own way in
the world.

High and assured status has obviously been very damaging to
those who possess it in this novel. In the first place, to be in a situation where one is constantly the object of envy and admiration tends
to produce vanity, a quality which is particularly characteristic of
Henry Crawford and the Bertram girls. But further, it is very
dangerous to be in a situation where bad behavior carries no sanc-
tions. Tom Bertram, for example, is in such a situation—when he is
extravagant, a living meant for his younger brother, Edumud, is
sold to pay his debts. If, like Tom, one need not make his way in the
world by his own efforts, if success does not depend upon one's good
behavior, then a powerful motive for behaving well is removed. It is,
the narrator remarks, "the consciousness of being born to struggle
and endure" (p. 473) that produces salutary habits of self-suppression and effort. For Jane Austen, good, active principle is a difficult
thing to live by since it often requires the sacrifice of personal desire,
and if one is merely "instructed theoretically in religion . . . but
never required to bring it into daily practise" (p. 463) by the circumstances of one's daily life, then it will probably be the case that
those theoretical principles will not take very deep root in the moral
character. And this is precisely what happens to the young people of
high status in *Mansfield Park*. Feeling that little or nothing of substance depends on their good behavior, they do not acquire the habit
of behaving well or the feeling that good behavior is vitally important. All that this group really need to do in order to maintain their
high social position is to live up to the fashionable code of propriety

that stresses elegance and polish of manner rather than true moral rectitude or even strict formality of the sort Sir Thomas tries unsuccessfully to impose on his family. This loose and corrupt code of good behavior—and we may see just how very loose it is by noting all the real immorality Henry Crawford gets away with in the early part of the novel without violating the code openly enough to attract general attention—is the only effective social check on this group of young people, the only external force operating to limit their freedom of action. And since the fashionable world's code of propriety, the code of "outs" and "not outs," is not especially moral in nature, this check does not generally prove a very galling one. Like Henry Crawford, Mary, Tom, Maria, and Julia may therefore all be said in part to have been "ruined by early independence," so that each frequently finds "the temptation of immediate pleasure too strong for a mind to make any sacrifice to right" (p. 467).

Further, a concomitant of low status which is still more important than low status itself in forming the moral character is the need to work for a living. The young Crawfords, as well as Tom, Maria, and Julia Bertram, occupy places in society where they are not only not required, but are practically not permitted to work. "To be distinguished for elegance and accomplishments" was "the authorized object" (p. 463) of the Bertram girls' youth, as it was of Mary Crawford's. Tom Bertram and Henry Crawford might, perhaps, have found some occupation in attending personally to the affairs of their estates, but nobody seriously expects this of them and Tom echoes society's expressed intentions for him when he feels "born only for expense and enjoyment" (p. 17). The young Prices, on the other hand, must work or starve; the girls are needed to help out at home, or if lucky, are taken on at Mansfield Park in semimenial capacities, while each of the boys must choose a profession at an early age. Edmund, too, must select a profession because he has no fortune. He chooses to become a clergyman and his advancement in this profession depends entirely upon his father, who intends to give him two excellent livings, but who also has extremely high standards, for that era, of the amount of work a clergyman ought to perform. " 'A parish,' " Sir Thomas remarks, " 'has wants and claims which can be known only by a clergyman constantly resident' " (p. 247). Hence Edmund has known from a very early age that his profession is not to be considered merely a sinecure.[9]

*Mansfield Park* might well be said to be Jane Austen's novel in praise of work, for in several ways work here has a consistently salutary effect on the moral character. Jane Austen, in this novel, considers morality to be in large degree a matter of habit—and the need to work forces one to acquire the habit of living up to an ideal of duty, a habit which makes principled action easier in other areas of life. Fanny, whose work is to serve members of the Bertram family in any and all capacities in which they choose to employ her, takes it as "a matter of course that she was not to have a moment at her own command" (p. 296) and is "totally unused to have her pleasure consulted, or to have anything take place in the way she could desire" (p. 280). These vocational habits have given Fanny another habit—that of repressing her own whims and desires on all occasions when they conflict with the needs of the family she serves, of struggling against herself in order to force her mind, her feelings and judgments, into conformity with the line of conduct which her vocational duties mark out for her. Fanny, and, in lesser degrees, her brothers and sisters and her cousin Edmund have acquired the essential moral habit which the leisured young people in the novel lack: the habit of struggling to live up to an ideal of duty. And this habit is gained almost entirely through the possession of a vocational role which absorbs time, energy, and feeling and which provides a standard of conduct. A social role which absorbs one's energies and to which one is emotionally committed can bring together the inner and outer aspects of character, providing a sense of self to which both one's principles and one's manners are integrally related. The social roles provided by the professions of Fanny, William, or Edmund are fairly satisfactory in this regard.

Further, the need to work prevents what is seen in this novel as a very great evil: the evil of having talents, energies, and feelings which lack the sort of healthy and satisfactory outlet that work can provide for them. This is precisely the situation in which Henry and Mary Crawford and all the young Bertrams but Edmund are trapped. We are told specifically that all these young people are intelligent, talented, and possess strong feelings, but these basically good qualities have, because of the more or less enforced idleness in which they live, been turned upon unsatisfactory and useless pursuits and have become corrupt. Feelings and talents, Jane Austen is saying here, must be employed, and if society fails to provide those feelings and talents with the sort of healthy vocational employment that will at least in part align them with feelings of duty, then they will probably employ themselves in pursuits of a highly dangerous nature. And this represents a departure from Jane Austen's point of view in earlier novels. In *Sense and Sensibility, Northanger Abbey,* and *Pride and Prejudice,* characters like Elinor and Marianne Dashwood, living in situations of enforced idleness, prove that they are basically worthy people by turning their leisure to good account—Elinor's art and Marianne's music, for example, show their ability to use leisure well. It is only in *Mansfield Park* that Jane Austen begins to consider the possibility that there may be some people with talent and potential who are unable to deal successfully with enforced idleness, but who might have turned out well had some absorbing pursuit been forced upon them.

Thus it seems basically to be low status combined with the need to work that is responsible for producing the principled young people of *Mansfield Park.* Jane Austen here asserts, unsentimentally, that virtue will become habit only if conditions force the individual to lead, from day to day, a principled, self-denying life, for the life of principle is not easy and requires constant sacrifice of self—and hence does not come naturally to anyone. It is low status—which makes good behavior a necessity—and an absorbing vocational role —which provides an individual with a sense of himself as subservient to a larger duty and prevents the evil of unemployed talents—that are the conditions of life most likely to have good effects upon the character.

Having a proper means of employing one's talents and feelings is very important in this novel.[10] If a young person, like the Crawfords and Tom, Maria, and Julia Bertram, is forced into idleness, the more talented and energetic he is, the more extreme is his danger. For his talents must find some outlet and if the conventional occupations open to him, like hunting, riding, polite conversation, music, drawing, or needlework, are not, as they are in the case of Lady Bertram, enough to exhaust his energies, then he will be restless and bored and probably will find for those energies a less socially acceptable and more dangerous outlet. And this is, of course, what happens to all the idle, talented young people in *Mansfield Park.* Lacking work to employ their talents, fill up their time, and give them a stable sense of themselves, these young men and women experiment with a variety of undesirable ways to exhaust their excess of feeling. Tom Bertram travels aimlessly about the country, seeking in changes of place and in new acquaintances the feeling of absorption which work would have brought him. His sisters, too, want to see new places and new people, to "find consolation in fortune and consequence, bustle and the world" (p. 202) for the lack of satisfaction within. But most of all Maria and Julia Bertram want to escape from the observation of their father, for he expects them to appear, and to be, fixed and stable characters satisfied with the limited amusements and duties of a respectable country gentle-woman—and he takes no account of the restlessness and dissatis-faction which they feel so strongly precisely because that situation bores them and fails to give employment to their energies and strong feelings.

Moreover their father, as we have noted, expects Maria and Julia to live up to a much stricter standard of propriety than that of the fashionable world—a standard to which they have not even the minimal internal commitment that they feel for the fashionable con-cept of decorum and which they see only as an intolerable restriction on their freedom of action. Maria thinks the rules of propriety that force her to treat her fiancé with minimal consideration are highly restrictive. She even equates them (half-seriously) with the tragic imprisonment of a caged starling which Sterne describes so pathet-ically in *A Sentimental Journey*. " 'I cannot get out, as the starling said,' " cries Maria (p. 99), referring explicitly to a locked park gate, but hinting at the restrictions of her engagement and of the rules of conventional propriety governing her behavior. This is the first hint of an impatience with even the minimal restrictions of the fashion-able world's code of propriety that will become significant later in the novel.[11]

Henry Crawford is, of course, the most talented and energetic of this group of young people and it is for this very reason that he turns out so badly. He has been totally independent and quite wealthy from a very early age and in "the riot of his gratifications" (p. 123) scarcely an untasted pleasure remains. Henry is bored not only with respectable pleasures, but also with the conventional dis-sipations which more or less satisfy Tom Bertram. He has, in short, exhausted nearly all the amusements open to a fairly honest young gentleman and is now trying some of the dishonest ones: in particu-lar, playing the lover to women for whom he cares nothing. Perhaps Henry has realized that the social role of an idle young gentleman will never satisfy him, for he occupies his talents in trying on, both in actuality and imagination, a variety of other roles. Thus we see him, in the course of the novel, acting the insincere lover to Julia and Maria Bertram, then doing his best to play the sincere lover to Fanny, and finally, when even that fails to satisfy completely, seeing what it's like to be a seducer. Lacking the sort of absorption and, more importantly, the self-definition which a vocational role would have assured him, Henry, with a sense of infinite possibilities before him, cannot decide either what he is or what he wants to be. When he listened to William Price describing his life at sea, Henry "longed to have been at sea, and seen and done and suffered as much . . . he wished he had been a William Price, distinguishing himself and working his way to fortune" (p. 236). It is sadly deflating, though hardly necessary, for Jane Austen to add that "this wish was rather eager than lasting" (p. 236), for it is evident that Henry's character has been fragmented and though he may wish to throw himself with ardor, once and for all, into some absorbing work, he is no longer capable of it. He may try on a variety of roles, but, unused to stability or satisfaction, he will never be satisfied. The vocational role which might have employed his talents and given him a fixed sense of the sort of man that he is has been lacking.[12]

Mary Crawford, too, suffers from restlessness and a similar sense of instability, though neither so poignantly, nor to the same degree. She too plays with the idea of committing herself to a different sort of life from the unsettled one that she has known. But though Mary considers marrying the poor man whom she loves as well as one of so unstable a character can love, the idea of giving up the excitements of London, ambition, and flirtation, and the employments which they provide for her lively talents, proves too much for her. Like her brother, Mary has no satisfying sense of herself and must always be adopting new roles. This seems finally to be the purpose of her humor and this is the reason why both Fanny and Jane Austen (who ordinarily loves nothing more than a laugh) disapproves so strongly of Mary's wit. For when Mary makes a joke she is always saying something either more or less or different from what she actually feels or ought to feel. Her humor enables her to try out various attitudes which intrigue her, but which it would not be acceptable or decorous to express seriously. When Edmund says of Mary, " 'She does not think evil, but she speaks it—speaks it in playfulness' " (p. 269), he is not entirely correct. Mary's playfulness enables her to experiment with attitudes of cynicism which interest her and to employ those lively talents of hers, for which she has no acceptable outlet, in a dangerous manner. Like Henry's downright deception of others or of himself, Mary's humor is seen as her experimentation with a variety of more or less unsatisfactory roles. Mary's humor represents a deviation from the integrity and sincerity which are the novel's moral ideals; [13] it is the result of light and lively talents which have not been properly employed and which have therefore become corrupt.

Mary, her brother, Tom, Julia, and Maria all have a sense of instability concerning their own characters and fates. Each is restless and unsatisfied, seeking and failing to find in new places, new ex-excitements, new attitudes, and new roles the sense of self-definition and contentment which the need to work has given Fanny, Edmund, and William and Susan Price. In the light of these considerations, Jane Austen's disapproval of the amateur theatricals in which these young people engage becomes easier to understand. True, the play is held to be wrong in a very prosaic light; the young Bertrams are all well aware, however much they may hope to conceal their awareness from themselves and each other, that their father would entirely disapprove of this amusement and that for that reason alone they ought not to engage in it. " 'I am convinced . . .' " Edmund says, " 'that Sir Thomas would not like it' " (p. 141). At issue here is one of those major rules of propriety—respect for parents—the moral validity of which Jane Austen does not question in this novel. But this is not, of course, the main reason why the evil which the play produces is dwelt upon so empathically. Jane Austen does not here disapprove of amateur theatricals in themselves—her censure is directed primarily toward the desires on the part of this group of young men and women which these particular theatricals will be employed to satisfy. For the theatricals are treated mostly as a symptom; but they are a symptom of the diseased state of mind of nearly all the young people of Mansfield Park.

Why are all the young Bertrams and Crawfords, with the exception of Edmund, so very eager to act and why, in particular, do they choose Mrs. Inchbald's *Lovers' Vows* as their play? One of the most important reasons for performing some sort of amateur theatricals is simply to keep busy and entertained. Tom Bertram, we are told, likes the idea of acting because he has "so much leisure as to make almost any novelty a certain good" (p. 123). But acting has the additional advantage of providing employment for some of those talents and tastes for which the young people can find no other satisfactory outlet. Tom Bertram is described as having "such a degree of lively talents and comic tastes, as were exactly adapted to the novelty of acting" (p. 123) and he states his own motive for acting to be a desire " 'just to vary the scene and *exercize our powers in something new*' " (p. 125, italics mine). All the young people are eager to be doing something that requires a degree of serious, steady application for its success—the sort of application which has been all too absent from their lives.

Another more sinister motive behind the desire to act is, as several critics have suggested, the idea of playing a theatrical role. Each of these young people is, as we have seen, restless and vaguely dissatisfied with his own vocational role in life and the scope for self-expression it permits him. Each hopes to find at least a temporary cure for this by placing himself mentally in the novel and interesting situation of a character in a drama. And in this respect the particular role which each chooses to play is a significant clue to the desires with which he is troubled. In the case of the love triangle formed at the time of the play by Julia and Maria Bertram and Henry Crawford, the choice of roles is especially significant. *Lovers' Vows,* a most inferior play, has been chosen. It contains two main plots: one concerns the fate of a fallen woman, Agatha Freiburg, and her illegitimate son, Frederick, the other concerns the growing love and eventual marriage of the young noblewoman Amelia and her tutor, Parson Anhalt. It is significant that Henry and the two girls who love him show absolutely no interest in playing the innocent young lovers, but are very eager to act the roles of the fallen woman and her son. This is partly due to the general preference these three young people have for the tragic mode, but it much more directly results from the fact that all three are interested in the illicit aspects of love, in the excitements of life outside the dull pale of society. By their desire to play the parts of Agatha and Frederick, Henry Crawford and Maria and Julia Bertram indicate that their restlessness and dissatisfaction have become very deep and corrupt indeed, and that they now wish to experiment with lives untrammelled even by the restrictions of the minimal code of fashionable propriety. Yet in the world of *Mansfield Park,* even the conventional propriety of the fashionable world is an important force. Virtue, principle, and a commitment to true propriety are, of course, the best guides to conduct, but they are all too often missing, especially in Sir Thomas's absence, so the purely social code of conventional propriety current in polite society is nearly the only limiting force affecting the behavior of these high-status young people—as little concerned with morality as that code is, its restrictions connect this group of characters with virtuous behavior more closely than anything else in their lives. As Mary Crawford puts it, " 'It is certainly the modestest part of the business' " (p. 50).

And it is precisely these limiting patterns enforcing a small but still restrictive degree of rectitude and modesty that the restless young people of *Mansfield Park* wish to transgress. When Edmund remarks that he " 'would hardly walk from this room to the next to look at the raw efforts [at acting] of . . . a set of gentlemen and ladies who have all the disadvantages of . . . decorum to struggle through' " (p. 124), he has unknowingly stated one of the main reasons why acting appeals so strongly to his young friends. Because they have no principles they yearn to escape the need to abide by those rules of decorous behavior which are theoretically supposed to be the outward evidence of good principles, and playing a theatrical role will make this possible in two ways. For acting a play provides all sorts of opportunities for dangerously frequent and intimate social intercourse and, further, allows one to try out what it feels like to be a character who is, in one way or another, free of the restrictions of polite society.[14] Thus we see that the young people of Mansfield wish to act for a variety of undesirable reasons: because they are idle, because they have no legitimate outlets for their powers, because they are dissatisfied with their own roles in life, and, worst of of all because, lacking principles already, they even wish to escape from the restrictions imposed by the merely fashionable rules of propriety. And this, of course, is always likely to happen when a person's code of propriety is not vitally connected to his moral principles and his sense of his own identity. We can imagine amateur theatricals undertaken in a very innocent spirit—for example, by some schoolchildren on holiday who have been excited by a Shakespeare play they have just read and wish to perform it—but at Mansfield theatricals are wrong because they are the symptom of a dangerous state of affairs and because they permit the fulfilment of several undesirable wishes.

The question of whether or not one possesses a set of principles is an important one in *Mansfield Park,* but principles are not, of course, either a simple or a complete guide to making moral judgments. In any decision which is moral in nature—for example, Edmund's decision to act—there are, in general, three elements which are operating. The first is the moral principle or principles involved—in our example, Edmund's belief that he ought to consult what he feels are his father's opinions on the subject and his belief that it would be dangerous to permit a stranger to become involved in the intimate social situation of the play. But moral principles are general and must be interpreted when they are applied to particular situations; further, they can conflict. In applying them, therefore, we must make a practical estimate of the particular situation with which we are concerned, so that we can see just how the moral principles in question fit in with it. Thus, Edmund concludes that his acting, though evil from one point of view, will probably keep his sisters and brother from greater evils of promiscuous intimacy and having their undesirable amusements discussed publicly. Actually, however, Jane Austen always considers a third element in the making of moral decisions: the element of feeling or desire. In any situation of moral choice the agent has desires concerning the outcome which are likely to bias his decision; Edmund's decision to act is biased by his desire to play opposite Mary Crawford.

Feeling can never, Jane Austen thinks, be eliminated from the process of making moral choices,[15] but feeling is a very unsafe guide to follow here. When Edmund remarks that, " 'Crawford's feelings . . . have hitherto been too much his guides. Happily, those feelings have generally been good' " (p. 351), he is wrong in two ways. First, of course, he is wrong because Henry's feelings have not generally been good, but second, and more important, because even good feelings can never be consistently good guides to morality. And this is precisely the point about moral choice which Jane Austen is making in *Mansfield Park*. Morality is a matter which involves the just application of impersonal rules to personal situations and insofar as personal desires enter the process of judgment, they can only distort it. If the rules, the principles, are good in themselves, and Jane Austen seems generally to believe here that conventional Christian principles are good in themselves, then they ought to be applied impartially. The principled characters in *Mansfield Park* seem conscious of this idea and they struggle to eliminate personal feelings as far as they can from their moral decisions, for they hope to base these on the surer guides of principle and practical evaluation of particular situations.

But naturally no one can ever succeed entirely in eliminating the element of feeling from the process of moral judgment. In this regard, the major characters in *Mansfield Park* form a continuum in the way they go about making moral decisions.[16] At one extreme of this continuum, we have Mrs. Norris. Not only is she totally lacking in principles, but she also almost totally lacks practical judgment as a basis upon which she can make her choices. Mrs. Norris has no idea of what the world around her is really like. She has created a world of imagination in which people correspond to what she wishes them to be—and this rarely has anything to do with what they are. Thus, she believes Maria, whom she loves, to be "perfectly faultless—an angel" (p. 39), and Fanny, whom she dislikes, to be lazy and sullen, "always lolling upon a sofa" (p. 71). With no principles and such wildly distorted vision, it is not surprising that Mrs. Norris makes morality the servant of her own desires; she does precisely as she wishes and thinks of some plausible reasons for it afterwards. When Mrs. Norris decides not to accompany her nephew and niece to Portsmouth, the real reason is that "it had, in fact, occurred to her that, though taken to Portsmouth for nothing, it would hardly be possible for her to avoid paying her own expenses back again" (p. 373), but her professed reason is that "she was a good deal too necessary to Sir Thomas and Lady Bertram for her to be able to answer it to herself to leave them even for a week, and therefore must certainly sacrifice every other pleasure to that of being useful to them" (p. 373).

And her views of propriety are as unreal as any of her perceptions. Because she wishes to degrade Fanny, Mrs. Norris believes that it would be improper for her niece, when she dines at the parsonage, to be " 'talking and giving your opinion as if you were one of your cousins . . . though Miss Crawford is in a manner at home at the parsonage, you are not to be taking place of her' " (p. 221). Actually, the rules of propriety dictate that Fanny, as the guest, must take precedence of the resident Miss Crawford, but Mrs. Norris (and in this she is unlike any of the other characters in the novel) fashions her code of decorum entirely to suit the wishes of the moment.[17] Mrs. Norris shows what happens when one is guided entirely by feeling—cut off from reality, without principles, she does nothing but harm.

Young people like the Crawfords, and Tom, Maria, and Julia Bertram are somewhat better off than Mrs. Norris in the way they go about making moral judgments. Like her they have no principles to guide them and hence their feelings are very important in determining what decisions they make, but unlike Mrs. Norris, they at least try some of the time to judge men and women as they are. They may often be wrong, but the fact that they make the attempt keeps them more in touch with reality than Mrs. Norris. When Tom Bertram wants to act he is able to convince himself that Edmund's objection that their father will disapprove is " 'Absolute nonsense! . . . Everything will be right with Sir Thomas' " (pp.

127-8). But even as he is making this remark, Tom doesn't entirely believe it, and when Sir Thomas returns unexpectedly, he finds that his heart is "sinking under some degree of self-condemnation . . . suggesting 'What will become of us? what is to be done now?' " (p. 175). Mrs. Norris, equally culpable, feels no such alarm, but Tom knows his father, though in his eagerness for pleasure he has chosen to disregard his knowledge, and is capable of realizing he has done wrong. Henry and Mary Crawford, as well as Tom's sisters, tend to behave similarly in situations of moral choice. In general they let their desires guide their moral choices and then think of whatever plausible reasons for those choices they can, but they have a knowledge of the world around them and a superficial commitment to conventional fashionable notions of propriety which prevents their actions from becoming, like Mrs. Norris's, totally severed from reality and their very feelings are truer to what is going on about them than hers ever are.

Sir Thomas is unique in the novel in the way he handles moral questions. He is a man of principle and he tries to live up to his principles, but throughout most of the novel, his attempt is by no means a great moral success for two reasons: his principles themselves are sometimes mistaken and he believes that he follows their dictates much more consistently than he actually does. Generally speaking, Sir Thomas' principles are not sound because they give excessive importance to position and money, even at the expense of human considerations. This is particularly clear in Sir Thomas's ideas about marriage. He believes that it is an evil for a young man to marry beneath him, no matter how deserving the object of his affections may be, and hence settles it in his own mind that neither of his sons may marry the indigent Fanny Price, before he has even seen her. In choosing a mate, Sir Thomas considers money and position, and even "county" and "interest" (p. 57), but love enters his calculations only as a very secondary matter. Thus, when contemplating his daughter Maria's match, Sir Thomas is able to calculate quite calmly the happiness which will be possible for "a well-disposed young woman who did not marry for love" (p. 201), and, incorrectly, concludes it to be ample. Now this sort of principle, in terms of which Sir Thomas, "a truly anxious father" (p. 19), makes his moral judgments, is obviously considered corrupt in the world of *Mansfield Park,* where money and status do far more harm than good to their possessors. At the end of the novel, Sir Thomas, by his conversion to a belief in the supreme importance of "the sterling good of principle and temper" (p. 471) acknowledges that the principles on which he has previously acted are not sound.

But though Sir Thomas' principles are not completely sound throughout most of the novel, they are partially sound and his greatest fault as a moral agent comes from the fact that he is tainted with unconscious hypocrisy and thinks he is living up to his principles much more rigorously than he actually is. Sir Thomas may value position and money too much, love too little, when he thinks about what makes a proper marriage, but theoretically at least, he believes some suitability of character and disposition between husband and wife to be a necessity. Thus Sir Thomas, wondering whether he should permit his daughter Maria to marry the imbecilic Mr. Rushworth, and desiring the match very strongly for worldly reasons, must convince himself that such suitability exists and is "very happy to think anything of his daughter's disposition that was favorable for the purpose" (p. 201), no matter how erroneous. This sort of self-deception is characteristic of Sir Thomas. The baronet considers himself, for example, "infinitely above scheming or contriving for even the most advantageous matrimonial establishment that could be among the apparent possibilities of anyone most dear to him" (p. 238), yet we see him devising a large number of schemes intended to forward the marriage of Mr. Crawford and his niece Fanny. It is for this reason that he seeks greater intimacy with the Grants, gives a ball at which Fanny and Mr. Crawford may dance together, leaves Fanny alone to cry over the cold pork bones on Mr. Crawford's plate after his farewell breakfast with her, postpones an interview between the two because he fears the effect Fanny's nose and eyes, red from crying, will have on her suitor, and finally, sends Fanny to Portsmouth to be starved into a juster value for Mr. Crawford's company. And his view of propriety, as we have noted, until his reformation at the end of the novel, is worldlier and more superficial than he himself believes it. Strictly decorous behavior is, for Sir Thomas, primarily a way of maintaining his own social superiority and keeping others in their places. Because he is never subjected to criticism from those around him (in part a result of his high status and the rigorous respect for that status which he invariably exacts), Sir Thomas, though he wishes to live up to his principles, finds it all too easy to let his desire for worldly aggrandizement guide his moral decisions, while he deceives himself and others as to the true nature of those decisions.

Fanny and Edmund usually make their moral choices in essentially the same manner. Like Jane Austen's other heroes and heroines, both Edmund and Fanny are people of strong feelings and desires. Even Henry Crawford notices that Fanny has "feeling, genuine feeling" (p. 235), and Edmund, too, is described as having "genuine strength of feeling" (p. 442). Presumably these strong feelings will influence Edmund and Fanny when they come to make moral judgments and this does, in fact, happen on many levels of subtlety and complexity. When Edmund lends the horse he has bought for Fanny to Mary Crawford, Fanny, unwilling to acknowledge that she is jealous, since she believes jealousy to be wrong, vents her anger by deciding, self-righteously, that it is "rather hard upon the mare to have such double duty . . . the poor mare should be remembered" (p. 68). Edmund, in love with Mary Crawford, tries to excuse or overlook her faults of character, while the jealous Fanny remains unusually clear-sighted, even for her, concerning those faults. In addition, Fanny, when Henry Crawford first proposes to her, has a fairly clear conception of what his character is like, but when she is lonely and forsaken in her squalid home at Portsmouth and he comes to visit her, her feelings are for the first time gratified by his affection and she therefore promptly decides that "he was much more gentle, obliging, and attentive to other people's feelings than he had been at Mansfield" (p. 406).[18]

The completely chaotic environment at Portsmouth, eternally in "confusion and noise again, the boys begging for toasted cheese, her father calling out for his rum and water, and Rebecca never where she ought to be" (p. 387), is the opposite of Mansfield's "elegance, propriety, regularity, harmony" (p. 391). Fanny is so completely distressed by the disorder, that she begins to overrate the importance of the purely external good manners that both the Bertrams and the Crawfords possess and value and to reject to some extent her earlier and more correct ideas on the true nature of good manners. Thus she decides that her uncle, because his behavior is decorous, must be "all that was clever and good" (p. 405) and that Mr. Crawford's character is wonderfully improved.

Fanny's nostalgia for the surface propriety, calm, and quiet of Mansfield, the value of which she has always overestimated, leads her to adopt some very mistaken views while at Portsmouth. She reflects that at Mansfield "everybody had their due importance; every body's feelings were consulted. If tenderness could ever be supposed wanting, good sense and good breeding supplied its place"

(p. 392). This is simply not so. Fanny herself has never had her due importance, nor were her feelings consulted, and the lack of tenderness at Mansfield is a serious flaw—hardly remedied by Sir Thomas' faulty ideal of good breeding. She is merely reacting to the "ceaseless tumult of her present abode" (p. 392) and refusing to recognise that the propriety of Mansfield also conceals real moral failings. Fanny's feelings here bias her judgment, as they do elsewhere throughout the novel, in the same way that Edmund's feelings often bias his judgment. In addition, however, Fanny's naiveté and lack of worldly experience—"He had said enough to shake the experience of eighteen" (p. 198), "Experience might have hoped more for any young people so circumstanced" (p. 367), and so forth—place her judgment under an additional disadvantage, one from which Edmund is comparatively free.

Fanny's moral judgment cannot be said to be a norm or ideal in the novel, in the sense that it is being presented as infallible, or nearly infallible as many readers and critics have felt. For Fanny's judgments, like Edmund's, are often at least partially mistaken, frequently biased by her feelings, and weakened in their authority by her inexperience. Yet the narrator rarely criticizes or takes an overtly ironic tone about Fanny's judgments. Perhaps Jane Austen's reason for having the narrator of *Mansfield Park* take such a positive view of Fanny is simply that she is well aware of Fanny's unattractive personality traits and since she wishes to prevent the novel's readers from disliking Fanny too violently, she permits the narrator to say everything that can possibly be said in Fanny's favor. For though Fanny's judgments themselves can never be accepted at face value as necessarily equivalent to Jane Austen's, Fanny's *method* of making moral choices, a method which Edmund alone shares, is indeed presented here as a norm. What distinguishes Edmund and, particularly, Fanny from all the other characters in the novel is that both realize clearly that feelings are not safe guides to moral choice and both, therefore, struggle to repress the personal element in order to make those choices in accordance with the dictates of principle alone. The key word here is "struggle"—because they have had to fulfil taxing vocational roles, both Edmund and Fanny have acquired salutary habits of self-suppression and as a result both struggle continually to prevent their principles from becoming the servants of their own strong desires. They certainly do not always succeed, but unlike the people surrounding them, they characteristically try and try hard. We repeatedly read phrases like "Fanny

checked the tendency of her thoughts as well as she could" (p. 424),
"Time did something, her own exertions something more" (p. 418),
"She must do her duty" (p. 331), "She tried to get the better of
it" (p. 303), "Fanny felt there must be a struggle in Edmund's
cheerfulness" (p. 273), and so forth—phrases which indicate that
Fanny and Edmund are both consciously engaged in a moral en-
deavor of great personal difficulty. Both Edmund and Fanny struggle consistently to live up to their principles and to the ideals of
propriety that are derived from those principles. Because their principles, unlike Sir Thomas's, are indeed sound, their moral decisions,
though far from invariably correct, are generally on the right track.

It is in this sense only that Fanny can be seen as a norm. Her
method of making moral judgments is conscientious and Jane
Austen endorses it emphatically here, but in spite of this her judgments themselves, like Edmund's, are seldom completely correct,
her feelings often not at all laudable. Readers who have disliked
Fanny are indeed right in thinking that she is timid, both self-
deprecating and quick to resent slights, inclined to be hard on
others, yet very regardful of how she appears to them. Fanny's
resentment and jealousy lead her to be consistently unfair to the
kindly and affectionate, if ill-principled, Mary Crawford, and her
timid care for the way she looks to others—"She began then to be
afraid of appearing rude and impatient" (p. 68), "Selfish and un-
grateful! to have appeared so to him!" (p. 321), etc.—is constantly
influencing her actions. Indeed, her care for the *appearance* of her
behavior to others even leads Fanny to agree to do the thing she
disapproves of most strongly in the first half of the novel: to act.
Asked to read the part of the absent Mrs. Grant at a rehearsal,
Fanny stoutly and self-righteously refuses until Edmund himself
begs her to give in "with a look of even fond dependence on her
good nature" (p. 172). Then, rather than appear ill-natured to him,
Fanny yields and is saved from the disgrace of participating actively
in the theatricals only by the opportune return of the disapproving
Sir Thomas.

For although Fanny is trying hard to behave well, her judgment
is so often biased by her feelings, which are not always pure, that
only her habitual passivity and unwillingness to do anything at all
"in propria persona" (p. 398) save her from being drawn into two
rather serious scrapes—as serious as the two major mistakes the more
active Edmund actually does make. She is almost persuaded to participate in the theatricals and it may well be only Henry Crawford's

elopement with Maria that prevents Fanny from ultimately yielding to the flattery of his addresses, as a result of her mistaken belief that his character has improved. It is only because Fanny is so consistently passive, that she is saved from acting wrongly almost as often as the equally well-meaning, but more decisive and energetic, Edmund.

Jane Austen expresses almost total approval of Fanny's method of making moral judgments—her struggle to repress the personal element—but treats her failure to repress it completely in almost every individual judgment she makes with gentle irony. Perhaps this discrepancy is responsible (along with the fact that Fanny's feelings are not, after all, always good, though her principles are) for much of the trouble her character has caused readers of *Mansfield Park*. Fanny, Edmund, and William and Susan Price have all, because of their rather low status and from the habit of working and living up to an ideal of vocational duty, acquired another habit of vital importance to good moral judgment: they struggle to repress feeling, to follow the dictates of principles and the rules of propriety that are derived from those principles, as far as it is possible to do so. And it is precisely this habit of struggle that the well-meaning Sir Thomas so tragically lacks. *Mansfield Park* is Jane Austen's novel in praise of hardship, work, and renunciation, of "the consciousness of being born to struggle and endure" (p. 473), and it is the novel's final irony to demonstrate, in the characters of Fanny and Edmund, that the struggle to see clearly and do one's duty, though laudable and necessary, will never entirely succeed.

# EGOTISM
# AND PROPRIETY
# IN *EMMA*

Of all Jane Austen's heroines, Emma Woodhouse is by far the most egotistical. "It is self-love," as Lionel Trilling remarks, that is her basic character trait. Her egotism always underlies and subtly influences the nature of the "energy and style and intelligence" [1] she exhibits. "A disposition to think a little too well of herself," the narrator tells us, radically understating the case, is one of the "real evils" (p. 6) of Emma's situation. Certainly Emma has an overly high opinion of and value for her own intelligence, the poise and polish of her social manner, her birth and wealth, and her insight into the feelings of others. Emma is always very conscious of the way she appears to those around her and hopes that they will value her, not merely at her own high estimate of her worth, but even more than she thinks she deserves. Thus Emma "was not much deceived as to her own [mediocre] skill either as an artist or a musician, but she was not unwilling to have others deceived, or sorry to know her reputation for accomplishment often higher than it deserved" (p. 44). Emma is so addicted to admiration and praise that she can enjoy it even when it is falsely conceived and incoherently phrased, as, for example, when Mr. Elton defends her portrait of Harriet from Mr. Knightley's just criticism that she has made Harriet appear too tall: " 'Oh, no! certainly not too tall; not in the least too tall. Consider, she is sitting down—which naturally presents a different— which in short gives exactly the idea—and the proportions must be preserved you know—Proportions, fore-shortening.—Oh, no! it gives one exactly the idea of such a height as Miss Smith's' " (p. 48).

It is not surprising that Emma should have an unrealistic opinion of her own abilities, or that she should demand constant admiration, for she has, virtually since birth, been the recipient of continual adulation from nearly everyone she knows. Mr. Knightley, "one of the few people who could see faults in Emma Woodhouse," is in fact, "the only one who ever told her of them" (p. 11). The continual adulation Emma has received from everyone else is partly the result of her high status as "Miss Woodhouse of Hartfield, the heiress of thirty thousand pounds" (p. 135). Partly, it is the consequence of her father's lack of critical ability—he is totally unable to correct and direct her as a parent ought. And partly it results from the fact that she is indeed more intelligent, lovely, and accomplished than most of her friends and neighbors. Emma's habitual dependence upon and need for continual assurances that she is wonderful in herself or superior to those around her is the character trait which determines a larger proportion of her opinions and behavior than any other.

At the start of the novel Emma is consistently portrayed as judging others almost entirely in terms of the way they affect her self-esteem. The most flattering relationship for Emma is one in which she is the recipient not merely of complete or almost complete approbation but also of a preference not accorded to any other person, and she responds very warmly to this sort of devotion. Emma's father, for example, must be an unbelievably trying man to live with, but Emma loves him tenderly and never resents him for a moment. Why? Because she is, as she herself accurately remarks, "always first and always right" (p. 84) in her father's eyes. Similarly, Emma seems unaware that her sister is a very tedious woman—hardly the "pleasant society" (p. 7) Emma believes her to be—and this is partly because Isabella is "so tenderly attached to her . . . sister that . . . a warmer love might have seemed impossible" (p. 92), and partly because Isabella, as Emma's sister, must necessarily be veiled with a corner of Emma's own mantle. The Westons too are peculiarly attached to Emma, and it is interesting to note that Emma's opinion of Mr. Weston begins to fall precisely when she realizes that he is as intimate with others as he is with her and reflects "that to be the favourite and intimate of a man who had so many intimates and confidantes, was not the very first distinction on the scale of vanity" (p. 320). It is only after feeling the effects of this ego-deflating revelation that Emma critically concludes that "a little less of open heartedness would have made [Mr. Weston] a higher character" (p. 320). Harriet Smith also is selected as Emma's friend at least in part because she feeds Emma's vanity every hour of the day. " 'Dear Miss Woodhouse, I would not give up the pleasure and honor of being intimate with you for anything in the world' " (p. 54) and remarks of similar nature are the staples of Harriet's "useful . . . conversation" (p. 69) with Emma. One reason why Emma selects Harriet, rather than Jane Fairfax, as a friend, is simply that Harriet has neither the inclination, nor the ability, to criticize her in the smallest particular.

But it is not merely by furnishing her with feelings of being preferred or admired that Emma's friends and acquaintances minister to her self-esteem, for Emma fancies herself as a manager of destinies and is kindly disposed toward those who permit her to use them as pawns. When, for example, she "makes" the match between Miss Taylor and Mr. Weston, Emma can congratulate herself on her insight into the hearts of those around her—and when Mr. Knightley informs her that she has merely made a lucky guess, she is quick to retort that " 'a lucky guess is never merely luck. There is always some talent in it' " (p. 13). Emma also congratulates herself on her managerial abilities. " 'If I had not promoted Mr. Weston's visits here, and given many little encouragements, and smoothed many little matters, it [the Weston match] might not have come to anything after all' " (p. 13), she tells Mr. Knightley. And, since Emma always believes herself to be managing others for their own good, she admires herself for her benevolence in taking the trouble to run the lives of her friends. Of Miss Taylor's marriage, Emma tells herself that she feels great "satisfaction in considering with what self-denying, generous friendship she had always wished and promoted the match" (p. 6). These three sources of the gratification which Emma's self-esteem receives from successful interference in the affairs of others are open to Emma herself as well as to readers of the novel; there is, however, a fourth source, probably more important than all the others, of which Emma is much less aware. For when Emma arranges the lives of others, she unconsciously, but very emphatically, reduces them to objects, beings whose existence has no particular justification except insofar as it helps display Miss Woodhouse's talent and virtue. By managing others, Emma convinces herself that she is a different and superior order of being and that she, alone, is responsible for her own actions and in control of her own destiny. Emma's attitude toward Harriet is striking evidence of this trait. From the very beginning of their friendship, Emma never accords Harriet fully human (or adult) status, always regards her as an object, in fact, as a toy. "A Harriet Smith, one whom she could summon at any time to a walk," "a valuable addition to her privileges," "exactly the something which her home required" (p. 26)—so Emma describes and redescribes Harriet in the space of half a page.

If the circle of Emma's acquaintances at Highbury is examined one by one, it becomes clear that virtually all of Emma's personal antipathies and preferences can be accounted for by the effects the person in question has upon Emma's self-esteem. Though Emma has often been called a snob, consistent snobbery—if defined as some sort of unvarying antipathy to all social inferiors who don't know their places or whose social habits seem vulgar to the person in question—plays very little part in her character.[2] Mrs. Weston, a former governess, and Mr. Weston, a man who has made only a very moderate fortune in trade and who comes from a family that is respectable, but has only recently become at all genteel, are, in Emma's view, of "the chosen and the best" (p. 20) society of Highbury, one of its "superior families" (p. 207). Speaking strictly in terms of social status and wealth, however, the Westons are, if anything, somewhat inferior to the Coles whom Emma holds in such contempt. Mr. and Mrs. Cole, too, derive their fortune from trade; their manners are less polished than those of Mrs. Weston, but they are also wealthier than the Westons and Mrs. Cole has never been forced to work for her bread. Therefore, if Emma regards the Westons as friends and the Coles as definite social inferiors, it is not mere social snobbery that is the cause. Emma loves the Westons for many reasons—Mrs. Weston is almost a mother to her and loves her very dearly, as does Mr. Weston, and further, both have been so obliging as to allow her to feel that she has made their marriage. Their whole relationship with her has made her feel good about herself and their purely social inferiority she (quite rightly, for once) ignores.[3] The Coles, on the other hand, are not peculiarly attached to Emma, for she scarcely knows them. However, as some of those undoubted social inferiors who form the social mountain of which Miss Woodhouse feels herself to be the apex, they have, in their humble way, had a good effect on her ego. And it is only when the Coles, grown as recently as in "the last year or two" so much richer as to be "second only to the family at Hartfield" (p. 207) in style of living, show a disposition to be recognized as social equals, that Emma, feeling threatened in a cherished sense of superiority, wishes to snub them and words her snub in such snobbish terms. Emma has a fixed view of how her acquaintances are—or ought to be—socially ranked, but this is determined not so much by the society's notions of wealth and status as by a set of highly idiosyncratic criteria which satisfy the needs of Emma's ego and the whims of her imagination.[4] For example, Emma's view that Robert Martin's social status is infinitely below Harriet's cannot be ascribed to simple snobbery. Emma is right in thinking that Robert Martin does not have the full status of a gentleman, but her reason for believing that Harriet must be a gentleman's daughter (because she " 'associates with gentlemen's daughters,' " i.e. with Emma herself, [p. 62]) results from overweening egotism alone. " 'My intimate friend,' " she unblushingly tells Mr. Knightley (p. 62), whatever her antecedents, cannot by definition be a fit match for a farmer. Strict snobbery would suggest that Emma ignore the illegitimate Harriet altogether, but Emma is willing to forego this snobbish gratification because her close friendship with Harriet flatters her complex sense of self-esteem in so many other important ways.

It is not difficult to demonstrate that Emma invariably judges others primarily as they affect her ego. Mr. Elton, though he is affected and incoherent, Emma at first regards as "really a very pleasing young man" (p. 35), partially because of his obvious admiration for her, admiration which she originally believes to be very humble and sincere, and partially because she intends to arrange his future for him and thinks that he will acquiesce in the arrangement. On the other hand, Emma dislikes Miss Bates and the whole reason for this cannot be found in Miss Bates's tediousness, for Emma's beloved father and sister are at least equally vapid, if not quite so verbose. Miss Bates admires Emma greatly, but it is always clear to Emma that Jane Fairfax, whom she regards as a threatening rival, holds the first place in Miss Bates's affection and esteem. The sort of admiration Miss Bates bestows on Emma—for example, at the Crown ball, " 'Upon my word Miss Woodhouse, you do look—how do you like Jane's hair? . . . She did it all herself. Quite wonderful how she does her hair' " (p. 323)—is neither focused enough, nor, more important, exclusive enough, to please one who is always so eager to be first. But Emma's interaction with Miss Bates is unsatisfactory primarily because it focuses so exclusively on Jane. Every time Emma sees Miss Bates, some ego-deflating reminder of Jane's superior virtues and accomplishments is "forced on her against her will" (p. 162)—and probably it is doubly humiliating to Emma that anyone so dull as Miss Bates should possess this power to unsettle her.

Emma's relationship with Mr. Knightley is, as might be expected, more complex, but it is not essentially different in kind from her relationships with other Highbury acquaintances. Emma respects Mr. Knightley's judgments, but she later realizes that she has previously been "insensible of half his merits . . . because he would not acknowledge her false and insolent estimate of her own" (p. 415). However, though Emma has often been annoyed with Mr. Knightley's refusal to approve and admire her every action, she also has always been aware that she comes *"first* with Mr. Knightley, first in interest and affection . . . feeling it her due she had enjoyed it without reflection" (p. 415). So the overall effect of Mr. Knightley's anxious concern for Emma's character and conduct has not been a displeasing one, since it has been a constant proof of her great importance to him. Though unaware that she loves him, Emma always knows that she likes and esteems him. With Mr. Knightley, as with her other acquaintances, Emma judges and reacts primarily, though not, of course, entirely, in terms of his effect on her sense of her own value.

The desire to feel proud of herself and superior to others is Emma's most basic character flaw, a flaw responsible, at least in part, for her desire to run the lives of her friends and for her poor judgment of some of them. This novel as a whole traces the improvement of Emma's character and judgment, a movement away from a desire to dominate, toward unpretending kindness, away from pride and vanity, toward humility and, most fundamentally, away from a tendency to judge others by their effects on her own ego, toward disinterested candor. Many readers feels that Emma makes only small advances in these respects by the end of the novel, but the direction in which she is moving is unmistakable.

Emma's pride is laid low in a good many ways in the course of the novel. Nearly every quality upon which Emma prides herself is proved either worthless or else something she does not possess to the degree that she believes she possesses it, and generally she has proved to be mistaken because of the overly personal and ego-bound way she judges people and values. How Emma views the nature and importance of elegant, socially proper manners, as this evolves and changes in the course of the novel, is a striking example of the way Emma is made to realize that a quality which is a source of pride to her is basically worthless. She has overvalued elegant manners precisely because she herself possesses them and so by overvaluing them can increase her feeling of self-esteem. The evolution of Emma's ideas concerning the nature of true propriety clearly illustrates Emma's typical, ego-centered mode of judgment.

At the opening of the novel Emma regards herself as a model of truly proper behavior and therefore she must form her concept of

what true propriety is in the image of her own behavior. Emma never formulates her concept of true propriety explicitly but her own social behavior and her reflections on the manners of her acquaintances demonstrate that she feels gentlemen and ladies ought to behave pretty much as she herself does. Emma is a mistress of the proprieties. She always handles social forms with great assurance and style. Emma is "never indifferent to the credit of doing everything well and attentively" (p. 24) on social occasions. She understands the minor rules of conventional propriety thoroughly and obeys them scrupulously. Whether in handing round the muffins or in paying civilities to the tedious Miss Bates, Emma is certain that her behavior is exactly what it should be. And when her companions displease her, as John Knightley does when he complains of the hardship of having to dine out at Randall's, or as Mr. Elton does when he prevents her from listening to a conversation she particularly wishes to hear, or as Miss Bates does when she describes Jane Fairfax's letter in minute detail, Emma derives a good deal of "comfort" from "appearing very polite while feeling very cross" (p. 119). Emma is always very pleased with herself for her polite forbearance toward the many people who annoy her repeatedly, because this forbearance places her, she feels, in a position of superiority: *they* may be rude, but *she* is invariably civil. The fact that she is always "feeling very cross" (p. 119) towards the recipients of this elegant courtesy, that her "civilities" are often paid to "a person she did not like" (p. 166), adds to, rather than detracts from, the value of her politeness in Emma's own eyes.

And this, of course, is the flaw in Emma's view of true propriety. She herself obeys the conventional rules to the letter, but she does so only because she wishes to *appear* ladylike and elegant to herself and others. Her deference to the minor rules of conventional propriety is not motivated by a sense of duty to others,[5] nor by commitment to moral principle,[6] nor even by the sort of generous feeling toward acquaintances that makes one wish to treat them politely or considerately. As we shall see, it is this last motivation that is the really important one in the world of *Emma*—but Emma herself does not exhibit it at all. Emma's everyday civility is not motivated by a desire to add what she can to the comfort of her acquaintances, but only by her own desire for "credit." Therefore, it is not surprising that Emma disregards the element of good feeling entirely in forming her tacit conception of true propriety. Since her feelings toward acquaintances are often hostile and are always colored by a large infusion of egotism, Emma must define her ideal of propriety in such a way as to exclude the element of good feeling if she is to continue to see herself as that ideal's embodiment. Emma does this by formulating an ethic of propriety that is more totally rule-oriented than that of any other major character in Jane Austen's novels. Emma's view of true propriety consists simply of strict outward obedience to the minor rules of conventional propriety.

Emma obeys the minor rules of propriety as invariably as Elinor Dashwood, but unlike Elinor, Emma gives these minor rules the primary significance in her code of propriety. In fact, Emma seems almost unaware that any rules of propriety can be more important than those minor rules governing such matters as handing round the muffins at Hartfield parties. Her concept of propriety focuses exclusively on the concept of "elegance," a concept which refers to style in handling the minor rules of propriety and ignores the major rules almost entirely. *Emma,* as its title suggests, is more completely a novel about its heroine and her problems than any of Jane Austen's others, and its themes are largely defined by Emma's own perceptions of reality. Hence, the propriety theme is defined here almost entirely as Emma herself perceives it. And since Emma means by good manners only outward fidelity to the minor rules of propriety, it is the true significance of those minor rules with which the novel as a whole is concerned. On those infrequent occasions when the major rules do come up (as they do, for example, in the case of Jane Fairfax's secret and improper engagement with Frank Churchill) their validity seems tacitly assumed. Emma's obedience to the minor rules of propriety is motivated purely by aesthetic and social considerations; that is, its purpose is to make her appear well-bred to herself or others. It serves no other moral or psychological purpose, has no other justification. In this it differs radically from Elinor's view of propriety in *Sense and Sensibility.* The outward sign of an inward commitment to an ideal of true propriety, for Elinor, is a strict obedience to the minor rules of conventional propriety similar to Emma's. But this external politeness means little to Elinor if it does not spring from a concept of duty—hence, Elinor doesn't have much use for the invariably proper, but mindless, lady Middleton.

Emma's own word for this tacitly held concept of true propriety is "elegance"—an idea which virtually obsesses her in the early sections of the novel. Since Emma's concept of elegance includes only those externals of social behavior in which she herself is letter perfect, her main interest is in evaluating the generally inferior style of her acquaintances' manners. Thus Harriet "wanted only a little more . . . elegance to be quite perfect" (p. 23). "Jane Fairfax was very elegant, remarkably elegant, and she had herself the highest value for elegance" (p. 167). Mr. Elton displays "a want of elegance of feature which she could not dispense with" (p. 35), and Emma later realizes that in his manners "true elegance was sometimes wanting" (p. 135). And as for Mrs. Elton, "neither feature, nor air, nor voice, nor manner were elegant" (p. 270), etc.

Emma's value, then, is for elegance and polish of manner. But propriety in the sense of kind, well-intentioned behavior, unadorned by grace of manner—which, as we shall see, turns out to be the standard of true propriety suggested by the novel as a whole—is not something to which Emma gives much thought. Her deeply ingrained egotism prevents Emma from reflecting that if polite behavior is supposed to be the outward manifestation of generous, kindly feelings toward others, but the feelings are actually hostile and cross, then a purely external decorum is not likely to save the situation permanently. According to Mr. Knightley, Emma imagines that Frank Churchill will exhibit the manners of a "practised politician, who is to read everybody's character and make everybody's talents conduce to the display of his own superiority" (p. 150). Actually, this is a fair description of Emma's own manners. For Emma, at the outset of the novel, propriety is a matter of ego and elegant outward demeanor, a question of appearing well in her own and others' eyes; she must learn that it is truly a matter of the heart.

When she meets Robert Martin, Emma holds a great many things against him—his low status, his comparative poverty, his lack of interest in such genteel fiction as *The Children of the Abbey*—and one of the foremost among her objections is that he is "so very clownish, so totally without air," that his manner displays an "entire want of gentility" (p. 32). "Gentility," here as elsewhere in *Emma,* means simply the code of propriety characterizing a gentleman or lady—but how *this* is to be defined is, as we shall see, a more complex question. Now Emma has previously observed that Mr. Martin's "appearance was very neat and he looked like a sensible young man" (pp. 31–2) and one would expect these considerations to vastly overweigh the fact that he "looked as if he did not know what manner was" (p. 32) in Emma's estimate of his character and potential. But no, Emma is sure that Robert Martin will develop, in a few years, into "a completely gross, vulgar, farmer—totally inattentive to appearances and thinking of nothing but profit and loss" (p. 33) merely because his manners lack polish. Further, Emma's opinion that this "neat" and "sensible" young man is entirely ungenteel reveals a concept of gentility which focuses exclusively on polish and disregards the elements of dignity, suitability, and internal worth which Robert Martin so obviously possesses. Indeed, Emma's original view of the Martin family is striking evidence of the high value she places on the externals of character—beauty, status, elegance (everything she herself possesses)—for the Martins display all sorts of solid worth, "good sense, warm attachment, liberality, propriety, even delicacy" (p. 51), but since they lack these externals, Emma holds them in undeserved contempt. It might be objected that Emma is here overstating the case against Mr. Martin for Harriet's benefit. And of course she is, but she is merely exaggerating objections to Mr. Martin which she herself really feels, not inventing arguments that she believes to be specious.

Now Emma's view of Mr. Elton is, as might be expected, the reverse of her view of Robert Martin in these respects. We learn in the course of the novel that Mr. Elton is insincere, ambitious, conceited, and even rather cruel, and we are given pretty fair evidence —evidence at all times available to Emma herself—of the existence of most of these traits from the outset. Yet Emma, until she receives decided proof to the contrary at the end of Volume I, continues to see Mr. Elton as "a most valuable, amiable, pleasing young man undoubtedly" (p. 111). Emma's striking misapprehension of Mr. Elton's character results in part from the fact that she intends to use him as a pawn in one of her managerial games, but an almost equally important cause of her mistake is her approval of Mr. Elton's gallant manners and her belief that they provide a trustworthy clue to his character and thoughts.[7] When Emma is trying to convince Harriet to transfer her affections from Robert Martin to Mr. Elton, she uses the superiority of Mr. Elton's manners as her main talking point (this perhaps betrays a feeling that Robert Martin is indeed the superior in most other respects). " 'I think a young man might be very safely recommended to take Mr. Elton as a model [of manners],' " Emma tells Harriet. " 'Mr. Elton is good-humored, cheerful, obliging, and gentle' " (p. 34). Now it is true that Mr. Elton's manners, gallant and conventionally reverent toward "woman, lovely woman" (p. 71), do indeed make ostentatious display of these qualities, but eventually it becomes clear that Mr. Elton actually possesses none of them. His irritability and self-pity after his hot and fruitless walk to Donwell Abbey show that he is neither good-humored, nor truly cheerful, his refusal to dance with Harriet at the Crown Ball is strikingly disobliging to Mrs. Weston, and his language when Emma rejects his proposal of marriage is anything but gentle. In fact, Mr. Elton's manners are radically at variance with the truth of his character and Emma, in regarding them as a reliable clue to that character, and a proof of his worth, makes in reverse the same mistake she made in her estimate of Robert Martin's manner and character. And so it is the excessive importance which Emma places upon the possession of an externally polished manner such as she herself displays that is in part responsible for the first major mistake she makes in the novel: her belief that Mr. Elton would be a possible husband for Harriet, as well as a husband preferable to Mr. Martin.

Mr. Elton's insolent proposal to herself shows Emma that he is "the very reverse of what she had meant and believed him" (p. 135), on the basis of his gallant and gentle manners, but her conclusion from this premise is a false one. Instead of concluding, as she ought, that elegant public manners are not always either an especially important virtue in themselves, or a good clue to the more important question of character, Emma merely decides that Mr. Elton's "manners . . . must have been unmarked, wavering, dubious, or she could not have been so misled" (p. 134). This is not really true—for though Mr. Elton's manners are ludicrous in their pretensions of sentiment and gallantry, those pretensions have always been aimed unambiguously at Emma herself—but it is an easy way out of her difficulty and Emma continues to retain her high value for a polished manner in spite of this incident. It will be a long time before she can see in Robert Martin "all the appearance of sense and worth which could bid fairest for her little friend" (p. 482), Harriet, in spite of his inelegant manner.

The next clue to the essential falseness of Emma's value for elegance is found in her ambiguous attitude toward Jane Fairfax. As J. F. Burrows notes,[8] on Jane's reappearance in Highbury, Emma is struck with the elegance of her looks and manner, so struck that she uses her favorite term to describe them no fewer than six times in the course of one page (p. 167). Emma believes that she herself has "the highest value for elegance" (p. 167), yet in spite of Jane's undoubted claim to that quality in all its aspects, Emma cannot really like her. She finds Jane "so cold, so cautious . . . disgustingly . . . suspiciously reserved" (p. 169). Emma does not, of course, realize that the frozen elegance, conventional propriety, and reserve of Jane's demeanor are defenses intended to protect the secret of her engagement with Frank Churchill, a secret which Jane feels to be continually threatened. But she does feel that there is something repellent in Jane's consciously proper manners and the element she misses in Jane is precisely the open and spontaneous display of sincere emotion. This feeling does not immediately set Emma thinking, but eventually, as we shall see, it does help her conclude that she has overvalued strict elegance and propriety as the essentials of good manners.

And another element in Emma's feelings which does not really correspond with her consciously held views of the nature of true propriety is her opinion of Mr. Knightley's unusual manners. On the whole, Emma thinks that Mr. Knightley's manners are good. " 'You might not see one in a hundred with *gentleman* so plainly written as in Mr. Knightley,' " she tells Harriet. Yet Mr. Knightley's manners are not, apparently, Emma's ideal: " 'if any young man were to set about copying [his manners] he would not be sufferable' " (p. 34), she remarks. Further, Emma never once uses that favorite term, elegant, to describe Mr. Knightley—and this is significant. For without realizing it, Emma has perceived that Mr. Knightley is a true gentleman, in the sense that he possesses the lofty, responsible, and generous feelings appropriate to the rank, but that he is almost totally uninterested in the polish of manner which has no necessary connection with those feelings. Mr. Knightley's feelings for others are generally very good, but he tends to ignore the minor ceremonies of propriety when he expresses them; as when, for example, he forces Miss Bates to give him a simple answer to a simple question by refusing "most resolutely and commandingly" (p. 244) to let her finish a sentence until she does so. Mr. Knightley wishes to make those with whom he deals as comfortable as he can—and he relies on his gentlemanly feelings to give him a truer guide to real propriety than the conventional minor rules of propriety strictly followed can provide. Mr. Knightley seems to think that neither the rules of propriety, nor even the concept of strictly factual honesty, is more important than his own generous gentlemanly impulses. It is the inward truth and propriety of his own feelings, not the externals of factual accuracy and conventional propriety, that matter to Mr. Knightley. It is interesting that though the other characters in the book regard Mr. Knightley as consistently "decided and open" (p. 460), disdaining "trick and littleness" (p. 397), he is, in fact, quite willing to scheme and even fib for what he regards as a good purpose. Thus, for example, Mr. Knightley persuades Mr. Woodhouse to go out for a walk, by remarking " 'I am going this moment myself' " (p. 58)—when his real intention is to get rid of Mr. Woodhouse so that he can enjoy a private conversation with Emma. Similarly, he convinces Miss Bates to accept a gift of his last barrel of apples by telling her that he still has a great many left. Mr. Knightley's idea of true propriety or gentility is simply that " 'English delicacy toward the feelings of other people' " (p. 149) by means of which the favored classes ought to repay the other orders of society for the privileges they enjoy. Part of the reason he is so severe upon Emma for her rudeness to Miss Bates is that Miss Bates is not Emma's " 'equal in situation . . . her situation should secure your compassion' " (p. 375). His remark that Robert Martin's " 'mind has . . . true gentility' " (p. 65), and that his unpolished manners are good manners because they have " 'sense, sincerity, and good-humour to recommend them' " (p. 65), shows that he has quite consciously formulated his concepts of gentility and propriety as primarily matters of thought and feeling.[9] But Emma criticizes Mr. Knightley for neglecting those externals of gentility which she values so highly. Mr. Knightley was "too apt, in Emma's opinion, to get about as he could and not use his carriage so often as became the owner of Donwell Abbey" (p. 213), carrying off his breaches of conduct with "an air of affected unconcern" (p. 214). We know, though Emma herself does not, that throughout the novel she admires Mr. Knightley more than anyone else she knows and the fact that his manners do not fit her own ideas of elegance or gentility is just one more indication that those ideas must undergo a change.

Emma's mistaken views of the importance of manner in Mr. Elton and Robert Martin and the revealing ambiguity in her feelings about Jane Fairfax's excessive elegance and Mr. Knightley's comparative deficiency of it are indications that the pride Emma takes in her own invariably decorous and polite behavior is going to be humbled. Until the question of Harriet's returning the call made upon her by Robert Martin's sisters arises, nearly halfway through the novel, Emma lives up to her own ideal of herself as the gracious, invariably polite great lady and does nothing that could even remotely be described as inelegant or rude. Indeed, as has been remarked, she has repeatedly been "positively civil" (p. 118) to people who have, at that very moment, been annoying her severely.[10] And it is only this marked discrepancy that can, up to this point, suggest to the reader that there may be considerations which will eventually prompt Emma to behave rudely, thus shattering an important aspect of her cherished self-image. The question of Harriet's call on the Martins gives the first hint that Emma's bad feelings may sometimes prove more powerful than her ingrained habits of conventionally polite behavior. Following an accidental meeting in a shop, Robert Martin's sisters have paid a formal call on Harriet. Emma well knows that it would be blatantly rude for Harriet to neglect to return this call, but she is afraid—and quite rightly—that a renewal of the close friendship which had previously existed between Harriet and the Martins will be very likely to end in the marriage of Harriet and Robert, a marriage which Emma has already done much to prevent. Emma's feelings are all in favor of keeping Harriet and the Martins strictly separated, but her habits of politeness will not allow her to dictate an openly rude course of behavior to Harriet. So Emma arrives at a compromise which, in actuality, is no compromise at all. "She could determine on nothing better than Harriet's returning the visit; but in a way that . . . should convince them that it was to be only a formal acquaintance" (p. 185). Superficially, the form of politeness will be preserved—the visit will be returned—but really Emma acknowledges "something of ingratitude merely glossed over" (p. 185) in the course of action she has chosen.

Although the forms of conventional propriety have superficially been preserved, Emma is not happy about the incident, concluding that "it was a bad business" (p. 187). The Martins, of course, deserve Harriet's gratitude and esteem, for they have been very kind to her, and Harriet ought to display that gratitude and esteem in the proper forms of social attention—in this case a long and friendly call. But Emma, who is determining Harriet's course of behavior here, does not have the respectful and grateful emotions toward the Martins which she ought, on Harriet's behalf, to feel. On the contrary, she resents them and feels threatened by their desires concerning Harriet's future. So, lacking the feelings which ought to prompt politeness toward the Martins and feeling such politeness to be dangerous, her habit of good breeding gives way and she directs Harriet to do what is in its essence, though not strictly speaking in its outward form, a rude thing. And here, for the first time, the bad feelings "merely glossed over" (p. 185) by conventionally proper behavior, which are so typical of Emma, make her feel uncomfortable and somewhat in the wrong. After Harriet's formal call on the Martins, indeed, Emma wishes nothing so much as to forget the entire affair. She "felt the necessity of a little consolation and resolved on going home by way of Randall's to procure it. Her mind was sick of . . . the Martins" (p. 187). And since Harriet is far from understanding the significance of the incident and Emma herself rarely encounters the Martins, she is soon easily able to put the whole perplexing and disturbing subject out of her mind. The lessons of Box Hill are still needed to prove to Emma how inadequate her ideas concerning the nature of good breeding are.

At Box Hill Emma learns, most definitively, that hostile, irritable feelings and elegantly courteous behavior—behavior prompted by a desire to look well to herself and others—are unstable companions. The Box Hill party as a whole displays that discrepancy between outward social forms and the feelings underlying them that Emma herself often shows in microcosm. "All the outward circumstances of arrangement, accomodation and punctuality were in favor of a pleasant party [at Box Hill]. Mr. Weston directed the whole . . . and everybody was in good time" (p. 367). Yet in spite of these smooth arrangements "there was a languor, a want of spirits, a want of union [among the party] which could not be got over" (p. 367). Emma herself is, of course, unaware that Frank Churchill and Jane, secretly engaged, have quarrelled, that Frank is paying attentions to her in order to make Jane jealous, that Mr. Knightley is very jealous of Frank and is avoiding his company by sticking closely to Jane and Miss Bates, and that Harriet, in love with Mr. Knightley, is depressed because he has not sought her out. The social forms to which she pays such great attention conceal all these hostile or sad feelings from Emma, who is aware only that the party is not going well and that she is not enjoying herself. And when Frank begins to flirt with her in a "talkative and gay" (p. 367) manner, she responds because she feels "less happy than she had expected" (p. 368) and hopes to cheer herself up. Soon Emma is indeed enjoying an exchange of superficial gallantries with Frank, gallantries that she well knows have nothing to do with their real feelings ("his attentions were not winning back her heart" [p. 368]), but which play cleverly with words and the social conventions of flirtation and provide Emma with a good opportunity to display the wit of which she is proud. As J. F. Burrows remarks, Emma's exchanges with Frank in this scene resemble the bright and artificial dialogue of Restoration comedy: [11]

"I am perfectly comfortable today."

"You are comfortable because you are under command."

"Your command? Yes."

"Perhaps I intended you to say so, but I meant self-command
. . ." (pp. 368-9),

and so forth.

Emma gets very caught up in this ostentatious display of wit,
but Frank has his eye on Jane and is determined to force her to
speak. So he tells the company at large that each one must think of
"'either one thing very clever . . . two things moderately clever,—
or three things very dull indeed'" (p. 370) to amuse Miss Woodhouse. And to this Miss Bates responds, "'Three things very dull
indeed. That will just do for me, you know. I shall be sure to say
three dull things as soon as ever I open my mouth, shan't I?'" (p.
370). Emma, still caught up in the atmosphere of the Congreve
dialogue in which she has just been participating—an atmosphere in
which wit, rather than good feeling or conventional propriety, is
the most admired quality—makes a witty, but rude (in spite of the
"mock ceremony of her manner" [p. 371]) and cruel reply. "'Ah!
ma'am, but there may be a difficulty. Pardon me—but you will be
limited as to number—only three at once'" (p. 370). The fact that
the narrator prefaces this retort with the remark, "Emma could not
resist" (p. 370), indicates that Emma senses she is openly violating
her own ideal of proper behavior in giving way to a temptation
which up to this time, however much Miss Bates has provoked her,
she has invariably resisted.

And why does Emma choose this particular moment to act in
so strikingly uncharacteristic a way? In part, of course, she is
unable to resist an appropriate, indeed an ideal, opportunity to put
down Miss Bates, for Miss Bates has always annoyed her as the
tedious and doting aunt of Jane Fairfax and every time she has seen
Miss Bates she has felt that "much had been forced upon her
against her will" (p. 162) by Miss Bates's loquacity, and all because of the civility she forces herself to display toward this boring
old maid. But though there is the release of accumulated annoyance
in Emma's rudeness to Miss Bates, a more important element is to
be found in the Restoration comedy setting where it occurs. Emma,
playing the role of a liberated female wit, Millamant to Frank
Churchill's Mirabel,[12] is carried away by the novelty of the thing,
and in her desire to shine in her new role she temporarily forgets
her old one: the gracious and elegant lady of the manor (or should

it be manner?). Emma's rudeness to Miss Bates points up most strikingly the dangers which have been inherent in Emma's typical practice of good breeding. Irritation and malice, such as Emma has always felt toward Miss Bates, are likely to break out in unguarded moments no matter how rigidly they are generally repressed by conventional rules of civility and good breeding. And further, if good breeding is prompted mainly by a desire to *appear* well-bred, rather than by the kind, forbearing feelings which ought to prompt it, there is always the possibility that the desire to appear polite will conflict with a stronger desire (as it here does with Emma's desire to shine as a wit) and will not carry the day. These dangers have always been real ones, though Emma has not acknowledged or considered them. And perhaps one of the reasons why Emma has never felt her position as a model of elegant decorum—in her own eyes and in the eyes of others—to be in jeopardy is precisely because that position is so very important to her.

Certainly, when Mr. Knightley makes his remonstrance—" 'How could you be so insolent in your wit to a woman of her [Miss Bates's] character, age and situation?—Emma, I had not thought it possible' " (p. 374)—both he and Emma are shocked at the unprecedented thing she has done and both regard it as in some degree incompatible with the image of Emma they have held. Emma, in particular, is deeply horrified. She suddenly realizes the falseness of that cherished source of pride, her good manners. She is upset "almost beyond what she could conceal" (p. 376) at Mr. Knightley's reflection that she has failed to fulfil the duties toward inferiors appropriate to her "situation" (p. 375), and that in fact she has not acted like a lady. This is a very novel circumstance for one who has heretofore been in such perfect control of her outward manner, but it is fitting that at the very moment when her externally polished manner fails her, sincere feeling should get the upper hand. Emma "had never felt so agitated, mortified, grieved at any circumstance in her life. . . . How could she have been so brutal, so cruel to Miss Bates. . . . Time did not compose her. As she reflected more she seemed but to feel it more" (p. 376). Why does Emma react so very violently to the realization that she has committed a single act of rudeness? She reacts violently because her image of herself as the ever gracious lady has been irreparably shattered and her vulnerable ego wounded at least as deeply as her conscience—"How could she have exposed herself to such ill opinion in anyone she valued!" (p. 376), she reproaches herself.

The shattering of this important prop upon which Emma's sense of self-esteem has rested, naturally destroys Emma's idea that true good-breeding and outwardly proper and polished manners are one and the same. No longer able to regard herself as a model of propriety, Emma, whose ego now as before plays a large role in directing her judgment, begins to amend her old definition of good breeding. Now she is ready to acknowledge and assimilate the lessons which her experiences with Robert Martin and Mr. Elton's manners, Jane Fairfax's excessive elegance and Mr. Knightley's want of it, and her own "polite" slighting of the Martins would have taught her earlier had her ego not been so very deeply committed to her own original view of the subject.

On the evening of the Box Hill party, Emma reflects, more consciously than she has ever done before, on the nature of true propriety. She acknowledges to herself that though her behavior has almost invariably been elegant and proper, her feelings have often been, in a perfectly defensible sense of the term, ill-bred. A true gentlewoman, as Mr. Knightley suggests, should be kind and forbearing and generous toward social inferiors, but Emma realizes that though she has been generous with the Hartfield pork, her feelings toward the Bateses have generally been so hostile as to display a notable lack of noblesse oblige. Emma admits to herself that "she had been often remiss, her conscience told her so; remiss perhaps more in thought than in fact, scornful, ungracious. But it should be so no more. In the warmth of true contrition she would call upon [Miss Bates] the very next morning, and it should be the beginning . . . of a . . . kindly intercourse" (p. 377). Having decided that her opinions and behavior have been seriously at fault, Emma reacts characteristically. First, to save as much as she can of her self-esteem, she reminds herself that though she has felt hostile and scornful toward some of her most deserving acquaintances, there are, nonetheless, important relationships in which her external propriety of behavior has indeed been backed by warm and generous feeling. "As a daughter she hoped she was not without a heart" (p. 377). Second, Emma resolves to begin immediately to live up to the new concept of propriety she has developed, so that she will again be able to appear estimable in her own eyes. Previously, Emma valued outward decorum and ignored gentle feeling; now she decides that where the feelings are good, appearances have only secondary importance. As she goes to pay her call on Miss Bates, Emma reflects that she may well meet Mr. Knightley on the way and tells herself that "she had no objection. She would not be ashamed of the appearance of the penitence so justly and truly hers" (pp. 377–8). Emma reflects also, as he climbs the Bates's stairs, on the difference between her new feelings and those she had always been conscious of on previous occasions. "She had never . . . before entered the passage . . . with any wish of giving pleasure, but in conferring obligation, or of deriving it, except in subsequent ridicule" (p. 378).

As soon as Emma gives up her belief that conventionally proper behavior is more important than proper feeling in social relations, she is free to elaborate a new ethic of propriety, one in which good feeling and plain speaking (qualities which have always characterized Mr. Knightley to a greater degree than anyone else in the novel) are the primary values. Like her old ideal of true propriety, Emma's new one is never formulated consciously or overtly. But it is easy to see from her own actions and from her occasional comments on the manners of her acquaintances that immediately after the Box Hill episode, Emma begins to emphasize the importance of openness and spontaneity. A concept that might be described as friendly truth replaces strict elegance in her scheme of values and in her idea of decorous, genteel behavior. Indeed, after Box Hill, Emma never again uses the term "elegant" except in a pejorative sense and the concept is abandoned to the possession of Mrs. Elton (whose "studied elegance" and "graciousness" [p. 321] have previously annoyed Emma as encroachments upon *her* territory) with the unstated implication that it has been suitable to her all along. Throughout the penitential call upon the Bateses which marks Emma's transformation in this regard, the narrator emphasizes the change in Emma's feelings and the new sincerity and spontaneity with which she expresses them. "Emma was most sincerely interested" (p. 379), "She spoke as she felt, with earnest regret and solicitude" (p. 380), "She sat musing . . . quite unconscious on what her eyes were fixed" (p. 384), "a repetition of everything that she could venture to say of the good wishes she really felt" (p. 384), and so forth. This is a very different Emma from the old hostile and controlled mistress of the minor proprieties, an Emma who actually wishes that others could see "into her heart" (p. 391) and who resolves that they should find nothing there of which she need be ashamed.

Emma is now free to admit to herself ideas she has been repressing all along. Mr. Knightley's manners, now that the concept of elegance is no longer in question, can be freely acknowledged as a norm, and in describing her new ideal of manners, Emma does in fact describe Mr. Knightley: "that upright integrity, that strict adherence to truth and principle, that disdain of trick and littleness, which a man should display in every transaction of his life" (p. 397).[13] Thus Emma's reëvaluation of the concept of true propriety brings her one step closer to admitting her own unrecognized love for Mr. Knightley. Further, Emma's rejection of elegance enables her to understand and resolve the ambiguity in her feelings toward Jane Fairfax. After the announcement of her engagement to Frank, Emma calls upon Jane, who, freed from the inhibiting effects of keeping her secret, is now able to behave with a "consciousness, animation, and warmth" of feeling (p. 453) which Emma finds "infinitely more becoming to her than all the elegance of her usual composure" (p. 459). Both young ladies, though for different reasons, are delighted to be freed from slavery to lifeless forms of propriety and both can now delight in speaking "more openly than might have been strictly correct" (p. 459). Emma takes leave of Jane in a glow of good feeling, enunciating her new ethic of propriety: " 'How much I love everything that is decided and open!' " (p. 460) and rejecting the cold and hostile politeness which has formerly marked her unsatisfactory relations with Jane.

Emma has come a long way. An ideal of propriety based purely upon externals has been replaced by one based upon the idea that speech and feeling ought to coincide. At the end of the novel, Emma wishes as fervently as ever to appear well to herself and others, but she is now concerned that those appearances rest upon reality. The narrator remarks that Emma "submitted quietly to . . . more praise than she deserved" (p. 475) when Mr. Knightley complimented her on having improved Harriet's character, but we know that she did not enjoy this praise and submitted to it only because she was afraid of betraying the secret of Harriet's love to Mr. Knightley. For to receive more praise than she deserves is no longer, at the close of the novel, a matter of pleasure to Emma, and this is a dramatic change. Emma's egotism has matured if not moderated, and her view of propriety has become more just—for egotism has been at the root of her view of propriety, as it has been at the root of so many of her opinions.

# PROPRIETY AND THE

# EXCEPTIONAL INDIVIDUAL:

# *PERSUASION*

In *Persuasion,* her last completed novel, Jane Austen reëxamines some of the most significant ideas about propriety which she had developed in earlier books. In *Sense and Sensibility,* as we have seen, Jane Austen considers the question of what moral considerations give both the major and the minor rules of propriety their authority over individuals in society. She concludes that the minor rules of propriety—those governing everyday social interactions— are justified because they provide a satisfactory guide to the sort of attention and consideration the individual owes to his fellows in society. The minor rules, in *Sense and Sensibility,* are viewed as the terms of a fairly just and workable social contract. And the moral individual must therefore obey them. The major rules of propriety —those regulating behavior at crucially important periods of life and defining the way the really significant social and familial re- lationships ought to be handled—are justified in *Sense and Sensibil- ity* on quite different grounds from those which are seen as justify- ing the minor rules of propriety. Jane Austen argues that these major rules codify the best ideas of past and present society concern- ing the handling of crucial, dangerous social situations in which in- dividual judgment tends to be uncertain. If, for example, Marianne Dashwood had obeyed the major rules of propriety dictating caution and reserve in the serious matter of courtship, her misjudgment of Willoughby's character would not have had so devastating an effect on her. In *Sense and Sensibility,* the major rules of propriety are there to protect Marianne and other people, both young and old, from the worst consequences of their own fallibility of judgment and the possible bad intentions others may have toward them. It naturally follows that only fools or devotees of foolish cults, like the cult of sensibility, will disregard these rules.

Thus, *Sense and Sensibility* defines true propriety as strict obedience to both the major and the minor rules of propriety. The only qualification of this statement which must be made is that external obedience to the rules of propriety constitutes true propriety in *Sense and Sensibility* only if the individual concerned is obeying the rules for the right moral reasons—and not merely, like Lady Middleton, because he wishes to appear well-bred, or from habit.

Unlike *Sense and Sensibility*, *Pride and Prejudice*, *Northanger Abbey*, *Mansfield Park*, and *Emma*, all treat the propriety theme in ways which do not seriously question the validity of the major rules. In *Pride and Prejudice* and *Northanger Abbey* the rules of propriety are divided into two classes: those rules which represent the social codification of society's moral values, and which must therefore be obeyed, and those rules which are purely matters of fashion or convenience and which therefore may sometimes be violated. Since the major rules of propriety all clearly fall within this first group, their validity is unquestioned in *Pride and Prejudice* and *Northanger Abbey*. In *Mansfield Park*, the validity of the major rules is merely assumed. When a character in *Mansfield Park* violates a major rule he does not (as in *Sense and Sensibility*) call the validity of that rule into question—he merely proves his own moral inadequacy. And in *Emma*, because Emma's own view of propriety focuses so exclusively on the minor rules, the question of the major rules is never really raised.

These four novels, then, do not challenge the defense of the major rules of propriety that Jane Austen suggests in *Sense and Sensibility*. They do, however, present ideas about the minor rules of propriety and the degree to which true propriety consists of obeying those rules to the letter, which are incompatible with ideas developed in *Sense and Sensibility*. Since the divergence on the question of the minor rules is greatest between *Sense and Sensibility* and *Emma*, we can examine the contrast between these two novels in order to see how Jane Austen's ideas concerning the minor rules changed between the time when she published *Sense and Sensibility* and the time she began work on *Persuasion*.

In *Emma*, Jane Austen develops the idea that what is really important in everyday social behavior is not, as in *Sense and Sensibility*, strict external obedience to the minor rules of propriety no matter how galling those rules may be to the feelings, but rather the presence of a spirit, the inward state of mind appropriate to gentlemen and ladies—regardless of whether that spirit does or doesn't express itself through external obedience to the minor rules of propriety. The spirit of gentility, Jane Austen feels, is one suited to a position of economic privilege, for it is a spirit of kindness and sympathy toward inferiors, courtesy and general good will toward equals, modesty and unaggressiveness where the self is concerned. In this view, the minor rules of propriety are merely the outward forms by which this spirit was, originally at least, supposed to be manifested. As forms, however, they are quite separable from the spirit they are supposed to demonstrate and, in some cases, may have ceased to represent that spirit altogether. Emma, for example, is able to maintain the minor forms of politeness in suggesting Harriet's ceremonious call upon the Martins, a call which is, in intention, a very rude thing. And having made this crucial distinction between the minor rules of propriety and that spirit of gentility which ought to animate the manners, Jane Austen is free to assign to the strict minor rules themselves a much less important place in the lives of moral individuals than she gave those same rules when she viewed them, in *Sense and Sensibility,* as a satisfactory guide to what the individual owes his fellows in society. Emma's own external propriety of behavior is treated as totally valueless because it does not spring from inwardly genteel, generous feeling. When, in *Sense and Sensibility,* Jane Austen sees the minor rules of propriety as the terms of a social contract, she holds those rules to be almost sacrosanct. But in *Emma,* where she views the minor rules only as approximate attempts to formalize an inward, emotional reality, Jane Austen argues that these formal rules can be dispensed with, when they fail to embody the feelings they ought to embody.

These two views of the minor rules of propriety cannot be completely harmonized, even if large allowances are made for the fact that Jane Austen was attacking a very different artistic problem in each novel. However, one of the things Jane Austen does in *Persuasion* is to give serious consideration to both these views at once, in a new artistic context. In addition, for the first time since *Sense and Sensibility,* Jane Austen here questions the value of the major rules of propriety as guides to social behavior. Perhaps it is because she realizes that her views concerning the minor rules of propriety have altered significantly since she wrote *Sense and Sensibility* that Jane Austen decides to reopen the question of the major rules in *Persuasion* to see if she still estimates their value as she did in *Sense and Sensibility*. In *Persuasion,* Jane Austen questions the view which she developed in *Sense and Sensibility,* that the major rules of propriety are justified because they represent the codified wisdom of past and present society, and hence are likely to suggest more efficient ways for the individual to behave in dangerous or very important social situations, than that individual could devise for himself.

The crucial difference between *Persuasion* and the earlier works is that it presents a more ironic and less doctrinaire view of the role that both the major and minor rules of propriety can and ought to play in individual lives than any of the five other novels. In *Sense and Sensibility,* for example, an important part of Jane Austen's attack on the cult of sensibility rests upon her argument that individuals need the rules of propriety as protection against the worst social consequences of their inevitable errors in judgment. And in *Emma* she uses her new view of propriety as genteel feeling fairly simply, as a way of exposing Emma's general hostility and her egotistical ethical standards. Only in *Persuasion* does Jane Austen give open consideration to all sides of the propriety question, examining both the possibility that the fallible individual may sometimes be wiser than the major laws of decorum and the possibility that trusting even the best feelings to determine the minor aspects of social behavior may not be an acceptable solution to the problem of how to promote true propriety. In *Persuasion* Jane Austen again examines the question: under what circumstances, if any, does an individual have the right to feel and act for himself in defiance of commonly accepted major and minor rules of propriety? And in this, her last detailed treatment of the concept of propriety, she is content merely to consider the problem in all its ironic and unresolvable complexity.[1]

Jane Austen began to write *Persuasion* soon after the completion of *Emma* and it seems probable that the themes of the former novel remained in her mind as she planned her new work. *Emma,* as we have seen, argues fairly unambiguously that good feeling is far more important than the letter of the minor laws of decorum as an aspect of true propriety. In *Persuasion,* Jane Austen by no means gives up the idea that there can be no true propriety without propriety of feeling, but she is now very concerned to examine some of the minute implications of that idea. In order to examine some of these implications, Jane Austen sets up three distinct groups of characters, each of which displays a different relation of inward feeling to outward propriety of behavior. In addition to these three groups, the

Elliot group, the Musgrove group, and the navy group, there are two characters, Capt. Wentworth and Anne, who stand alone and, as outsiders, are able to reflect upon the behavior of each group and its implications.

The Elliot group—composed of Sir Walter, Elizabeth Elliot, Mr. Elliot, and Lady Russell—is remarkable for the strict propriety of its outward behavior and the emphasis its members place upon the importance of conventional, polished, and elegant manners. Sir Walter and Elizabeth, ridiculous though they are as personalities, possess a set of "public manners" in which even the fastidious Anne finds "nothing to blush for" (p. 246). Mr. Elliot's manners are "rational, discreet, polished" (p. 161) and he lives "without defying public opinion in any point of worldly decorum" (p. 146). And Lady Russell is "most correct in her conduct . . . with manners that were held a standard of good breeding" (p. 11). But though all the members of the Elliot group are careful to obey the minor rules of conventional propriety to the letter, they are also—though in varying degrees—deficient in those generous and kindly feelings which ought to prompt truly decorous behavior. Sir Walter and Elizabeth are complete egotists; the proper behavior of each is prompted only by the desire of "being known, by report, . . . as a model of good breeding" (p. 32) and for acquaintances who do not in some way minister to their sense of self-respect, they feel little but contempt.[2] Their view of propriety is so very much an affair of externals that they have no objection to behaving with downright rudeness—as Elizabeth does when she cuts her old acquaintance Capt. Wentworth on first encountering him at Bath—provided they are fairly certain of not being found out by the world in general. Mr. Elliot is that rare bird in Jane Austen's works, a truly conscious hypocrite, and he manipulates his command of the proprieties so as to deceive others concerning his true intentions—paying, for example, just enough attention to Elizabeth Elliot to keep her from observing his deeper interest in Anne. Lady Russell, of course, is a more sincere person than Mr. Elliot and a more generous and reasonable one than Sir Walter and Elizabeth, but she nonetheless resembles this unattractive trio in that she regards outwardly proper behavior as very important, but doesn't worry much if proper feelings are lacking. Thus, when Anne tells her about Capt. Wentworth's courtship of Louisa Musgrove, Lady Russell gives herself full marks for the fact that she can decorously "listen composedly and wish them happy" and does not reproach herself because "internally her heart revelled in angry pleasure, in pleased contempt" (p. 125) that Capt. Wentworth had confirmed her low opinion of him.

In their various ways, this rather contemptible group of characters demonstrate that proper manners are valueless if they are not accompanied by proper feelings, that outward elegance is a worthless quality.[3] The consciously polished behavior of Sir Walter and Elizabeth is as far from making them, as they suppose, irresistibly attractive, as it is from producing the ease and good feeling fine manners are supposed to create. Their entrance into a room seems "to give a general chill" and their "heartless elegance" (p. 226) puts an end to all comfortable communication. Lady Russell's manners, since they are not so radically divorced from her feelings, have better success, but her excessive value for outward decorum leads her to make two serious mistakes. "Capt. Wentworth's manners had not suited her own ideas," so Lady Russell had concluded him to be of dangerous character, and "because Mr. Elliot's manners had precisely pleased her in their propriety and correctness," she had received them as evidence of a "well-regulated mind" (p. 249). These mistakes, of course, come perilously near to wrecking Anne's happiness and further, Lady Russell's feeling that all communications ought to be made within the bounds of propriety prevents Anne from making Lady Russell a real confidante during her eight years suffering. So the Elliot group prove that a value for good manners at the expense of good feelings and a belief that polished manners are certain evidence of those feelings are self-defeating as grounds of behavior and dangerously uncertain as grounds of judgment. The only thing that can be said for the Elliots' commitment to proper manners is that without it they would be even more odious than they are with it. The need to be well-bred does place a check of sorts on their behavior and hence cannot be completely despised.

The value which the Elliot group places on propriety of manner is closely related to the group's characteristic method of judging the worth of individuals. This focuses almost exclusively on external attributes such as manners, inherited status, appearance, and, in the case of Lady Russell and Mr. Elliot, wealth. None of these attributes have any necessary connection with the sort of internal worth that is measured by intelligence and good feeling (though of course it is possible that a man like Capt. Wentworth will be wealthy because he is intelligent and active, or a woman like Anne will display good manners which are truly the result of generous, warm feelings).

This tendency to judge by the externals alone—hardly even realizing that if the externals are valuable it is primarily as signs of something else—betrays the Elliot group's essentially inhuman scheme of values, a scheme which makes the individual's public self infinitely more important than his private worth. The Elliots and Lady Russell damn their own set of values completely when they seek the company of the stupid Lady Dalrymple and Miss Carteret, although this pair are admittedly "nothing in themselves" (p. 150), merely because they possess the external attributes of "birth and good manners" (p. 150). Taken to extremes, this attitude results in Sir Walter's reduction of human beings to names: "'A widow Mrs. Smith—and who was her husband? One of the five thousand Mr. Smith's whose names are to be met with everywhere'" (p. 157), he remarks of this worthy woman. By associating the Elliot group's value for good manners with its more obviously ridiculous and dehumanizing value for beauty, status, and money, Jane Austen shows her readers how ludicrous it is to value fine manners when one does not value the good feelings those manners are supposed to express and reminds them again that true propriety cannot be merely a matter of obeying the minor rules of propriety.

Having examined, in the Elliot group, the case for propriety divorced from good feeling and found it wanting, Jane Austen goes on to examine the Musgrove group, who are characterized by a general willingness to break the minor laws of propriety in a manner which the Elliots would find unthinkable. The Musgrove group —composed of Mr. and Mrs. Musgrove, Louisa, Henrietta, Charles and Mary Musgrove—by no means so totally lacks the good feelings which ought to stand behind proper behavior as the Elliot group, but neither are the Musgroves' feelings precisely those which Jane Austen would describe as truly genteel. Though they are in general warmhearted and generous (this does not, of course, apply to Mary, who is more of an Elliot in this regard), the Musgroves are also limited in their knowledge of the world, not particularly perceptive of character or motive, rather narrow in their sympathies, and infected by the restlessness and boredom arising from idleness of which Jane Austen so deeply disapproves. So in her examination of the Musgrove group, Jane Austen considers what happens if fairly ordinary people choose to obey the dictates of their feelings rather than the laws of strict propriety.

The most interesting example of how the Musgroves are willing to disregard the minor laws of propriety is found in the improper style of their social life at Uppercross. The Elliot family mansion, Kellynch Hall, is the abode of excessive formality, where even Sir Walter himself invariably refers to his daughter as Miss Elliot, while the Musgrove village of Uppercross has dispensed with most of the rules intended to govern day-to-day social life. Polish is out of the question; in fact, the Musgrove habits are "not at all elegant" (p. 40). Further, the Musgroves possess few resources for amusing themselves except casual socializing and they have "more dinner parties, and more callers, more visitors by invitation and by chance than any other family" (p. 47). However, even this does not suffice to occupy the time of the two Musgrove families, so they fill in the blank by maintaining with each other a close intimacy which is not governed by any of those minor rules intended to set a genteel tone, encompassing both good feeling and a sense of privacy, in such relationships.[4]

The results of this willingness to break the minor rules of decorum, from the dictates of feelings which are not particularly genteel or laudable in nature, are mixed. Anne, always the best judge of right and wrong in *Persuasion,* considers the Uppercross style of social intercourse "highly imprudent," for she realizes that the excessive intimacy there produces "continual subjects of offense" (p. 40) in both families, of precisely the sort that the minor rules of propriety, by keeping people at a distance from each other, are designed to avoid. Each family is affected by and conversant with the most minute details of the behavior of the other family, and this encourages interference and friction. Anne finds this improper intimacy "one of the least agreeable circumstances of her residence" (p. 44) with the Musgroves. We are given a dull and puzzlingly long catalogue of the quarrels in which the Musgroves ask her to interfere and this catalogue seems intended as evidence of how very annoying breaches of propriety made in the wrong spirit can be to innocent bystanders.[5] But though Anne finds the Musgroves' improper and imprudent style of intimacy personally trying, she realizes that "neither family could now do without it" (p. 40), for it serves their needs as individuals better than truly proper social intercourse ever could. And, of course, the Musgroves' good-hearted spontaneity is both more attractive and closer to the ideal of true propriety than is the Elliot group's cold-hearted decorum.[6] Thus there is something to be said for allowing even those who are not motivated by the feelings of true gentility to break some of the minor laws of decorum. The rules may generally be wise, but they

do not necessarily serve the needs of the ordinary man, whose unwise desires often demand satisfaction even at the expense of rational
comfort. And this is a consideration which was not raised in Jane
Austen's earlier novels.

It is the navy group of characters—composed of Admiral and Mrs.
Croft and Capt. and Mrs. Harville—which most closely approxi-
mates the ideal, suggested in *Emma,* of manners based not upon an
excessive respect for the minor laws of propriety, but rather upon
generous, kindly, sensitive feelings, feelings which are by nature
truly genteel, but which may demand expression in ways that are
not always strictly decorous. Mrs. Croft is an extremely attractive
and sensible woman, but she—like the rest of the navy group—is
not really elegant. "Her manners were open, easy, and decided, like
one who had no distrust of herself and no doubts of what to do"
(p. 48), manners, that is, characterized by self-reliance rather than
conformity to the minor rules of decorum. And, in order to distinguish Mrs. Croft's manners from those of the Musgroves, the
narrator is quick to add that her behavior, unlike theirs, is quite
"without any approach to coarseness . . . or any want of good
humor" (p. 48). Mrs. Croft, however, is too intelligent not to be
highly aware of how important many social conventions are, though
she cares little for polish or strict formality, and she is careful to
prevent her less intelligent and more impulsive husband, Admiral
Croft, from committing many small breaches of propriety which
may prove disquieting to his associates. For if Admiral Croft, at
a formal dinner party, feels in want of exercise, he thinks nothing of
taking "two or three refreshing turns about the room with his hands
behind him" until he is "called to order by his wife" with a reminder
that it is neither the time nor the place for a brisk walk. Indeed, the
narrator gives a sufficient description of Admiral Croft's impulsive
and informal manners when she remarks that they "were not quite
of the tone to suit Lady Russell" (p. 127), that devotee of elegance.
In the description of Capt. and Mrs. Harville, the remaining members of the navy group, one notices something in the narrator's tone
indicating that they are not of quite as high a social class as the
other major characters. We learn that they are poor, and not particularly well educated, and that they live in a very humble way.
However, the narrator firmly assures her readers that Capt. Harville, however inferior to the other characters in birth or wealth,
is "a perfect gentleman" in essentials, not elegant, but "unaffected,
warm, and obliging" (p. 97). Mrs. Harville is "a degree less polished"

even than her husband, but displays "the same good feelings" (p. 97). The Harvilles, in fact, are so little connected with the sort of elegant society in which the minor rules of propriety are vitally important, that they have no sense of how odd their casual manners, based on their warm feelings, look to one who, like Anne, has been raised amid affluence and social polish. The Harvilles can unembarrassedly invite the whole large Musgrove family to dine with them in "rooms so small as none but those who invite from the heart could think capable of accommodating so many"—though even the sensitive Anne feels "a moment's astonishment" at the ignorance of the "usual style of dinners of formality and display" (p. 98) which such an invitation betrays.

The members of the navy group live in a social commonwealth of their own making where feelings of warmth and discriminating friendliness tend to dictate manners. And since the feelings which dominate here are so very good, so truly genteel, in their essence, the arrangement works very well indeed and exercises "a bewitching charm" (p. 98) upon the intelligent outsider who, like Anne, has been raised in a more formal world. We must recall the incredible dullness of the Elliots' world of forms—"it was but a card-party . . . a mixture of those who had never met before and those who met too often—a commonplace business, too numerous for intimacy, too small for variety" (p. 245)—to appreciate the value of this unconventional social commonwealth. The members of the navy group in *Persuasion* are Jane Austen's natural aristocrats of feeling and, through them, she indicates her belief that this sort of aristocrat can be permitted to make his own laws (though, of course, she assumes that, being sensible people, these characters will not often want to break the more basic rules of propriety).

Only in the character of Admiral Croft is a hint given the reader that even manners based upon real good will might sometimes be improved by a respect for the minor laws of decorum. For the perceptive Mrs. Croft sometimes seems slightly afraid that her husband's informality may prompt him to indiscretion or may even make others uncomfortable. When, for example, Anne makes her first visit to Kellynch Hall after the Crofts have rented it, the admiral rather distresses her by his insistence that she should "not stand upon ceremony—but get up and go over all the rooms in the house" (p. 127) and by his innocently unguarded reflections on her father's character: " 'He must be rather a dressy man for his time of life—Such a number of looking glasses' " (p. 128). Jane Austen seems here to be giving no more than a gentle hint that even warm, generous feelings may sometimes need control, and that if a fine intelligence does not supply this control—as it does in Mrs. Croft—some attention to strict propriety may be desirable as a substitute. That she did not want to make this point too strongly is proved by the cancelled chapter of *Persuasion,* which contains an incident where Admiral Croft does indeed ignore the minor laws of propriety to such a degree that Anne finds herself "very much distressed. She knew not what to do or what to expect" (p. 256) from the admiral's improper impulsiveness. I think that Jane Austen eliminated this section of the manuscript in part because she did not wish to imply that Admiral Croft's manners could really be so highly objectionable to Anne as she portrays them in this chapter when she has previously made it clear that the admiral's "intentions are always the kindest and the best" (p. 257) Such intentions, Jane Austen probably thought upon rereading this chapter, are not really consistent with the sort of embarrassingly persistent impropriety she had portrayed, even though the point had previously been made that the admiral tends to live a bit too much in a world of his own making. For the navy group of characters generally demonstrate that intelligence and warm generous feelings can, in large measure, be trusted to know when to obey and when to disregard the minor rules of propriety and the drawbacks of this procedure—which the character of Admiral Croft so gently indicates— are likely to be minor.[7]

Capt. Wentworth, like Anne, cannot be classified as a true member of any of these three contrasted grougs. During most of the action of *Persuasion,* Capt. Wentworth is a disappointed and dissatisfied man, still smarting from Anne's rejection eight years before and engaged in a doomed attempt to fall in love with another woman. Thus, though he shares the navy group's general informality of manners, his feelings, warped by disappointment, are not so consistently fair and generous as those of his contented fellow officers. When Capt. Wentworth's feelings are good, as they are, for example, toward the Harvilles or Capt. Benwick, his manners are perfect and his disregard for the rules of propriety and prudence are endearing and laudable. When, for example, he rushes off to console Capt. Benwick on the death of his fiancée, Fanny Harville, Capt. Wentworth does not even wait for official permission to leave his ship and we all think the better of him for this disregard of the constricting demands of law and prudence. But when he is under the sway of his less likeable impulses—for example, his anger toward Anne (which influences so many of his judgments and feelings), or a sort of general contemptuousness toward happy, ordinary people, which his own disappointment seems to have produced (demonstrated, for example, by his contempt for Mrs. Musgrove's exaggerated sorrow or his unwillingness to use his ship to convey the wives of other naval officers to join their happier husbands)—his lack of strict decorum appears to less advantage. The "curl of his handsome mouth" (p. 67) which demonstrates his contempt for others and which Anne notices repeatedly, though a "transient . . . indulgence of self-amusement" (p. 67) nonetheless expresses the fact that Capt. Wentworth lacks self-control and a proper respect for good manners, that he allows himself to express his bad, as well as his good, feelings in action. And when Capt. Wentworth is touched on a raw point—as he is when Anne is forced to leave the task of nursing Louisa at Lyme to her sister Mary—his impulsiveness becomes downright rudeness. "His evident surprise and vexation . . . the change of his countenance . . . the expressions begun and suppressed . . . made but a mortifying reception of Anne" (pp. 115–116) when Capt. Wentworth suspected her of being unwilling to help, for his sake, to care for Louisa. He hurt Anne's feelings deeply and unfairly by his unguarded behavior.[8] Capt. Wentworth is, of course, a man who believes in self-reliance and he is not, on principle, willing to submit to being trammelled by the petty minor rules of convention any more than he was willing to obey the dictates of prudence in giving up his engagement with Anne. But in view of all the bad—and often unfair—feelings which he so impulsively expresses, the reader is left with the idea that, in the absence of better feelings, a greater respect for the minor rules of decorum would make Capt. Wentworth a truer gentleman—though, of course, when at the end of the novel he is reunited with Anne and his feelings improve, Capt. Wentworth's manners benefit from the change.

Capt. Wentworth's ideas on the question of manners are doctrinaire. The other characters in *Persuasion* (except Anne and Lady Russell) behave in the manner most natural to them and think little about it, but as a result of his disappointment in love, Capt. Wentworth has become an advocate of firmness as a rule of conduct, and an aspect of his idea of firmness is the ability to disregard both the major and the minor rules of propriety where they conflict with an individual's strong desires or purposes. Anne, on the other hand, though she often reflects on the question, is not really a consistent adovcate for any one particular view of manners. Standing, like

Capt. Wentworth, outside all three groups of characters, but, unlike him, living to a large extent in isolation, she is able to reflect sensitively and perceptively on the relationship of manners and feeling, a question which she cannot completely resolve. Anne, of course, knows the members of the Elliot group, with the exception of Mr. Elliot, very well and she is repelled by the "elegant stupidity" (p. 180) of her father and sister's idea of good manners. And just as she repelled by her own family, so Anne is attracted by the informal good feeling which characterizes the navy group and which promises her the sort of warm human communication she knows only, and only to a degree, with Lary Russell. Reflecting upon Mr. Elliot's polished and controlled manners, Anne hints at a bold speculation concerning the relationship of feeling and conduct: "Mr. Elliot was . . . not open. There was never any burst of feeling. . . . This, to Anne, was a decided imperfection. . . . She prized the frank, the open-hearted, the eager character beyond all others. . . . She felt that she could so much more depend upon the sincerity of those who sometimes looked or said a careless or a hasty thing, than of those whose presence of mind never varied, whose tongue never slipped" (p. 161).

What Anne seems to be implying here is that the minor rules of decorum are bound, at least at times, to conflict with the impulses of the truly feeling individual and therefore those individuals who can manage to behave decorously at all times ought to be suspected either of lacking feeling or of having repressed feeling to the point where it is hardly worthy of the name. Thus, Anne sees the minor rules of propriety as prescriptions which, if followed too closely, are likely to destroy spontaneity of action and finally even spontaneity of feeling itself, which may ultimately warp the individual's moral character. And she reserves her deepest approval for those who demonstrate sincerity by an inability to be completely decorous at all times.

But though Anne makes these speculations tentatively and though she is most unambiguously charmed by the warmth and spontaneity of the navy group, she herself, though a warm and feeling woman, is unable to behave impulsively and can, generally, be described as a model of strict conventional propriety. Anne never consciously reflects that she herself does not exhibit the spontaneity of manner she most admires, but in fact of all the novel's attractive characters, she alone is described as elegant: "the elegant little woman of seven and twenty, with . . . manners as consciously right as they were invari-

ably gentle" (p. 153). And Anne never commits a real breach of
propriety, in spite of the fact that her sufferings, as she bears slights
and injustices with perfect decorum, are often severe. Are we therefore meant to accept Anne's stoical and painful commitment to the
minor rules of decorum as an ideal superior to the navy group's
freer sort of behavior? I do not think we are. Anne, it is true, is a
person of good feeling, fair and generous, but there are two important reasons, neither of them especially to her credit in a moral sense,
why she has developed a deeply rooted habit of behaving with strict
propriety however much the necessity galls her feelings—a habit
which has become so automatic to her that she is scarcely even aware
of its existence. First, Anne, despite her mental superiority, has been
raised as an Elliot and though her more mature judgment has
rejected most of the Elliot values, she has apparently found it more
difficult to alter the habitually decorous demeanor which, presumably, she was taught as a child, than she has to reject the Elliot idea
that status and beauty are the important elements of human worth.[9]
Second, and more importantly, Anne has just passed eight unhappy
years during which she has been forced to conceal the deepest feelings of her heart for everyone around her. And in this concealment
the minor rules of propriety have been a great aid to Anne, for they
have enabled her to interpose a conventional and impersonal mode
of behavior between the world and the secret she must conceal. In
her isolation of feeling, Anne has habitually used the minor rules of
propriety to conceal her feelings and motives. She is always being
"obliged to turn away, to rise, to walk to a distant table, and, leaning
there in pretended employment try to subdue the feelings" (p. 160)
she wishes to conceal from her companions, to plead indisposition to
escape from unwanted social engagements, to wait for information
to be offered rather than to ask it, to distort the truth, if not actually
to lie, in order to manage her father and sisters, and so forth. In
fact, if Anne feels she can only trust the sincerity of those who
behave with some impropriety, she may in part be reacting to the
radical disparity she often senses between her own feelings and her
invariably proper behavior. Circumstances and training have forced
Anne's manners to be, at least on some occasions, nearly as false to
her feelings as are the manners of the hypocritical, deceitful Mr.
Elliot, despite the fact that her motives are infinitely superior.

And just because Anne is the most sensitive and reflecting individual in this novel, we are not necessarily meant to accept her
stoical manners as an ideal. On the contrary there are definite signs

that, as Anne, at the end of the novel, regains Capt. Wentworth's love and moves toward a position in which she can express her deepest feelings more freely, her manners become more impulsive, less strictly elegant. When she realizes that Capt. Wentworth is again in love with her, she tries to encourage him actively, modifying the strictly passive and correct modesty of demeanor which has previously distinguished her and which has served so well to conceal her anguish of heart. When Mrs. Smith teases her about her supposed engagement to Mr. Elliot, Anne, not without a struggle, feels compelled to hint, though to do so is indecorous, that she has another lover. Anne regrets her indiscretion "with a deep blush" (p. 197) but realizes that to have told Mrs. Smith less would hardly have been honest. And, indeed, it is this uncharacteristic breach of a minor rule of propriety in favor of friendly communication that encourages Mrs. Smith to reveal Mr. Elliot's true character to Anne. Similarly, Anne's last breach of propriety has the good effect of producing more open communciation between herself and her lover; in fact, it emboldens Capt. Wentworth to make his proposal. For when Capt. Harville begins to speak to her of constancy in love, she responds to the warmth of his feeling for her by being honest and unguarded about her own deepest feelings in a way that would have been unthinkable for the frozen, repressed Anne of the first half of the novel and that is not strictly decorous, considering how slight her acquaintance with Capt. Harville actually is. The signs that Anne's manners are becoming freer and more impulsive, though unambiguous, are few and slight, for Anne has been raised as an Elliot and her eight years of sorrow have made self-control and suppression of feeling so much her automatic response that no dramatic change can be expected.[10] I think that we are intended to feel that Anne's early training and long unhappiness have destroyed—not her feelings, which have, if anything, been strengthened by sorrow and repression—but rather her power of expressing them spontaneously.

As *Persuasion* draws to a close, Anne becomes more impulsive, but she will never be able to emulate the self-reliance and warmth of the navy group whose manners she finds so "irresistible" (p. 127) and who are so easily able to establish the sort of warm and open friendships for which Anne longs, but which her repressed feelings to some extent make impossible. Whether Anne consciously wishes to alter her own style of manners is very doubtful; nevertheless her manners in terms of the entire novel, cannot be seen as an ideal, since they do not further the sort of open human relationships which Anne and most of the other estimable characters in the novel need more than anything else. Anne does in fact change in the course of *Persuasion,* though slightly, in the direction of greater informality of manners, and to the extent that she is unable to break through her habits of strict propriety, we are, I think, meant to see her as the unfortunate victim of a formal upbringing and the crippling need to protect a secret. In terms of the relationship of manners to feeling, it is Mrs. Croft or Capt. Harville, and not Anne, who is at the center of the novel. Anne and Capt. Wentworth are both somewhat lacking in this respect—Anne bound too strictly to the letter of the minor laws of decorum, Capt. Wentworth too willing to ignore those laws. The manners of each suffer from the emotionally damaging effects of their misfortune in love. He—the believer in self-reliance—expresses his feelings too freely, she—the isolated sufferer—not freely enough (especially considering how good her feelings are). As the novel closes, Anne and Capt. Wentworth approach each other more closely, but to some extent their characters remain complementary and it is in their marriage, rather than in each as an individual, that the true balance of feeling and rule is struck.

Jane Austen's examination, then, of how strictly one ought to obey the minor rules of propriety when those rules conflict with one's feelings, is a complex one, but the emphasis of the novel as a whole is on the charms of good feeling freely followed, and in terms of this emphasis Anne's manners cannot be seen as representing an ideal. Moreover, Jane Austen does not, in *Persuasion* as a whole, endorse Anne's beliefs concerning the major rules of propriety as correct. Critics who, relying on the narrator's tone of warm affection and approval toward Anne, have concurred wholeheartedly in Anne's final judgment that she was right in obeying the dictates of prudence and the major rules of propriety in breaking off her engagement with Capt. Wentworth, have been forced to be rather ingenious in justifying a decision which seems to pull in the opposite direction from the rest of the novel. A close examination of the complex way *Persuasion* treats how the major rules of propriety relate to and govern fallible individual judgments will, I think, clarify this point by showing that, whatever the narrator's tone toward Anne may imply, the heroine's opinion on this matter is not totally trustworthy.

Jane Austen states the conventional view of the relationship between the major rules of conduct and the individual judgments they are supposed to aid simply and straightforwardly in her account of Capt. Wentworth's simultaneous courtship of Henrietta and Louisa Musgrove. Capt. Wentworth is, as we have seen, an advocate of individual discretion in the matter of manners, for he believes that both the major and minor rules of decorum dictating prudence and caution in human relationships are basically mistaken and inimical to human happiness. " 'My first wish,' " he tells Louisa Musgrove, " 'for all, whom I am interested in, is that they should be firm' " (p. 88), that they should, in other words, make up their own minds on matters of conduct even in defiance of convention. And Capt. Wentworth has, in fact, gotten so completely into the habit of judging even major questions of propriety by his own standards that, during the first half of *Persuasion,* he can, in conventional terms, behave most improperly almost without being aware of it. It is in this individualistic frame of mind that, wishing to marry, Capt. Wentworth meets the two attractive Musgrove girls. Flattered by their admiration, he seeks a close intimacy with both in order to discover whether he will be able to fall in love with either. Capt. Wentworth, used to setting his own standards, seems innocently unaware of the impropriety of his behavior, but Anne, always so conscious of the rules of decorum, is unwillingly forced to conclude that he is "wrong in accepting the attentions . . . of two young women at once" (p. 82). The elder Musgroves who, as we have seen, are not models of propriety themselves, seem as unaware of the danger of Capt. Wentworth's behavior as he is himself, apparently feeling "an entire confidence in the discretion of both their daughters and of all the young men who came near them" (pp. 74–75)—a confidence which the facts do not justify. And in Capt. Wentworth's romance with the Musgrove girls a good many of the major rules of propriety governing the important matter of courtship are indeed violated without "the smallest appearance of solicitude or remark" (p. 75) on the part of those directly involved.[11] Propriety and prudence dictate that Capt. Wentworth should not court two sisters at once, and that if he does do so their parents should interfere; and when Henrietta withdraws from the picture, the major rules of decorum state that Capt. Wentworth should not be nearly so particular in his behavior to Lousia as he is, unless he feels very certain that he wants to marry her.

These major rules of propriety are, of course, intended to prevent young girls from falling in love with or expecting offers from young men who do not intend to marry them, as they are intended to protect young men from getting themselves into positions where they are forced in honor to marry women whom they do not love. These rules represent socially approved and time-tested ways of dealing with the problems of courtship in accordance with society's moral values. But Capt. Wentworth disregards these major rules from conviction and anger, and the Musgroves from a sort of short-sighted good-will. The resolution of this group of people (none of whom, though for different reasons, can judge clearly) to rely on their individual judgments rather than upon the wisdom of society very nearly brings them to lasting grief. Henrietta is fortunate that she has Charles Hayter to fall back upon when Capt. Wentworth decides he prefers her sister, fortunate also that she hadn't really fallen in love with this dashing officer. But when, at the very moment he learns he does not love Louisa, Capt. Wentworth is "startled and shocked" (p. 242) by the discovery that his friends consider him an engaged man, his agony of mind is severe. He suddenly realizes that: "'I was no longer at my own disposal. I was hers in honour if she wished it. I had been unguarded . . . I had not considered that my excessive intimacy must have its danger of ill-consequence in many ways; and that I had no right to by trying whether I could attach myself to either of the girls, at the risk of raising even an unpleasant report, were there no other ill effects. I had been grossly wrong and must abide the consequences'" (pp. 242–243). And only the fantastic piece of good luck which Louisa's engagement to Capt. Benwick represents for Capt. Wentworth saves him from being forced to marry a woman he does not love purely as a result of his ill-considered disregard of those major rules of decorum precisely intended to prevent such a contretemps. In this episode, as in *Sense and Sensibility,* the major rules of propriety are proved to be a useful aid to the fallible judgments of individuals not particularly well qualified to judge for themselves, with only, perhaps, the sly reservation that luck plays such a large role in human affairs that it may sometimes negate the effects even of serious misjudgments—particularly when the individuals involved are as easy to satisfy as Henrietta and Louisa Musgrove.

Against the gross misjudgments of the unintelligent Musgroves and the angry Capt. Wentworth, the major rules are vindicated; but in answering the question of whether the finely sensitive Anne should have obeyed the major rules of propriety dictating prudence and obedience to elders, in breaking off her engagement, Jane Austen considers a much more complex and ambiguous aspect of the relation of rules to individual judgment. Two of Anne's character traits are of paramount importance here. The first is her strong commitment to all the rules of propriety inculcated by her unbringing as an Elliot—and it is indeed hard to see why the first three chapters of *Persuasion* should be devoted to such a very detailed description of the Elliot family character if not to give readers a clear picture of the home which has formed Anne. And in addition to possessing something of the Elliot respect for proper appearances, Anne also perceives clearly, though her father and sisters do not, that both the major and minor laws of propriety are often closely related to the laws of morality, a perception which naturally increases her commitment to the rules and her desire to obey them even in those instances where she doubts their wisdom. Thus when Anne, reunited to Wentworth at the end of the novel, tells her lover that " 'I should have suffered more in continuing the engagement than I did even in giving it up, because I should have suffered in my conscience' " (p. 246), readers remembering her strong habits of moral and social correctitude, will doubtless agree that for Anne, the worst sort of suffering would come from breaking the rules in which she believes and which it is almost an emotional necessity for her to obey.

The second aspect of Anne's character which must be taken into account in evaluating her decision to renounce her engagement is her very unusual degree of perceptive insight into the human heart. "There is a quickness of perception in some," the narrator of *Persuasion* remarks, "a nicety in the discernment of character, a natural penetration, in short, which no experience in others can equal" (p. 249) and it is Anne who possesses more of this insight than any other character in the novel. This is not, of course, to say that Anne is never wrong in her estimates of worth and motive—she often is, especially when she tries to penetrate the state of Capt. Wentworth's feelings toward her, a matter in which her own feelings are too deeply involved for her judgment to be quite as reliable as usual. The assertion is merely that Anne can penetrate beneath those externals of manner which here tend to conceal the realities of character with a very unusual degree of accuracy. We are not justified, however, in concluding from Anne's subtlety of insight during the action of *Persuasion* that she was equally perceptive eight years earlier. On the contrary, we are, I think, meant to believe that the enforced isolation and suffering in which Anne has lived have given her improved insight into the human heart—but that she has always been, to some degree, unusually sensitive and perceptive, we are not meant to doubt.

Here, then, is the problem: a young girl possessing at once a very strong commitment to standards of strictly proper conduct and an unusual insight into character and motive, an insight which often makes her individual judgments superior both morally and psychologically to those based on conventional wisdom and the laws of society, is forced to make a crucial choice between major rules of conventional propriety and the promptings of her own intellect.[12] Two major rules of propriety are involved in Anne's decision to break her engagement with Wentworth. The first of these is a rule which governs parents—or those who, like Lady Russell, stand in place of parents—when their daughters enter into engagements which, for financial reasons, are likely to be protracted indefinitely. It is a major rule of propriety that parents should advise their daughters to break such engagements. This principle is not, perhaps universally accepted as an unambiguous rule, but the fact that all three of the novel's fairly sensible adult women characters, Lady Russell, Mrs. Croft, and Mrs. Musgrove, agree unhesitatingly (p. 231) that they would act upon it, indicates that its acceptance as a principle of conduct is widespread.[13] And Lady Russell does, in fact, act upon this major rule of propriety in advising Anne to break her engagement with Wentworth.

Now this major rule of propriety makes several tacit assumptions concerning the feelings which may be true of people in general, yet be quite untrue in any individual case. The most important assumptions implicit in the rule might be stated as follows: first, it is assumed that the young lovers involved, if they do not remain formally engaged, will become free enough in feeling to make more prudent marriages within a reasonable period of time: second, it is assumed that if they should in fact remain in love with each other and one of them should become wealthy enough to marry, they can renew the engagement. Now actually neither of these plausible and socially sensible assumptions—the precise assumptions made, of course, by the conventional and unperceptive Lady Russell in advising Anne to break off her engagement—applies at all to the unusual love affair between Anne and Capt. Wentworth. For eight years later neither one of the lovers has been able to forget the other (though Capt. Wentworth deceives himself in this respect) or to enter into a more prudent engagement with someone else (though Anne, and presumably Wentworth also, has had this opportunity).

Further, Capt. Wentworth has been so deeply hurt by Anne's prudent rejection of him, so unable to comprehend her true motives
(which were, of course, "for *his* advantage," [p. 28]), that he cannot
bring himself to renew their engagement, though he still loves her,
when he becomes rich enough to marry. Thus Lady Russell's conventional advice does not really, as Anne herself later supposes, fall
into the category of "one of those cases in which advice is good or bad
only as the event decides" (p. 246), advice depending, that is, for its
justification on the question of whether the couple involved would
have been lucky enough to obtain the means to marry fairly quickly.
Capt. Wentworth was financially lucky and could have married
Anne after a fairly short interval, but this is not really the issue. For
even had Capt. Wentworth remained a poor man most of his life,
he and Anne would still have been happier in continuing their engagement—setting aside, for the moment, Anne's sense of guilt—
simply because their feelings for each other did not depend on the
formality of an engagement. Neither lover could, as conventional
wisdom and the major rules of conventional propriety in which it is
embodied suppose, be restored to freedom of heart by the termina-
tion of their formal betrothal. So far from restoring to them the
freedom to improve their worldly prospects by financially profitable
marriages, Anne's decision to end her imprudent engagement locked
both herself and her lover into a condition of permanent estrange-
ment from each other without ending their love, a condition of
perpetual suffering infinitely worse than any that would have been
involved in the most vexatiously long engagement or in an impecu-
nious marriage.

Lady Russell, the essence of conventional wisdom, judged conventionally when she concluded that such an engagement as Anne and
Wentworth's was undesirable. Anne, however, with her superior
perception, knew that it was not. Yet she allowed herself to be
persuaded and, in later years, though she regretted the advice Lady
Russell had given her, did not regret her decision to follow it. " 'I
was,' " she tells Capt. Wentworth, " 'perfectly right in being guided
by the friend whom you will love better than you do now. To me
she was in the place of a parent . . . I have now, so far as such a
sentiment is allowable in human nature, nothing to reproach myself
with; and if I mistake not, a strong sense of duty is no bad part of a
woman's portion' " (p. 246). At issue here is a second major rule of
propriety. At the end of *Persuasion,* Anne states that it was in some
sense her "duty" to accept Lady Russell's advice to end her engage-

ment and the source of this duty is to be found in the major rule of propriety which states that the young have an obligation to be guided in crucial situations, for their own good, by the wisdom of the experienced. This is indicated by Anne's use of the words "being guided by"—rather than, for example, "submitting to" or "obeying" —to describe her reasons for acting on Lady Russell's advice. Indeed, the idea that Anne should have given up her engagement to please or obey her surrogate mother, Lady Russell, or her father is never even hinted at in the text. Anne follows Lady Russell's advice because "she was persuaded [by it] to believe the engagement . . . indiscreet, improper, hardly capable of success," a bad thing both for herself and for Capt. Wentworth (p. 27). Therefore the duty, the major rule of propriety, in question here seems to be founded upon the assumption that age is the best advisor for youth—and this, as we shall see, is the very assumption that Anne's unusual perceptiveness calls into question.

At the end of the novel, though Anne realizes that Lady Russell's prudent and proper advice to her was based on mistaken assumptions—conventional assumptions which, however justified in general, did not apply to the love between herself and Capt. Wentworth— and though she was resolved that she should never "in any circumstances of tolerable similarity, give such advice" (p. 246), Anne still accepts the need for and general rightness of the major rules of conduct. Of course, it can be said that a sense of duty is no bad part of a woman's portion because without such a sense society would degenerate into chaos, and perhaps this is a part of what Anne means. So Anne, at the end of the novel, reaffirms her belief in the Elliot value for convention (though she defines convention more intelligently than her family does) and this reaffirmation, especially in the light of Capt. Wentworth's ill-fated attempt to ignore the major rules of propriety, seems persuasive.

Yet the thought lingers—and I think Jane Austen intended it to do so—that Anne, so sensitive and perceptive about people, was always better qualified to judge for herself than the conventional wisdom of society as codified in its major laws of propriety was to judge for her. It is the duty of young people to respect their elders' advice on the important question of marriage because experience is presumed to have given older people a better ability to judge that complex question. But Anne's judgment has always been superior to Lady Russell's as well as to her father's. Anne is at once the individual to whom the conventional psychological assumptions underlying the major laws of propriety do not apply and the unusual intellect which is capable of judging and managing particular situations more effectively than any general rules of decorum can do. The Musgrove family ignores the major rules of propriety through ignorance of the danger of what they are doing, and Capt. Wentworth believes himself much better qualified to judge those rules for himself than he actually is, but Anne does indeed possess wisdom superior to the codified wisdom of society, a subtle perceptiveness which is repeatedly demonstrated in the course of *Persuasion* and which—along with her warmth of feeling—constitutes a major portion of her charm as a heroine. Anne's sensitivity is of great importance both in the scheme and interest of the novel and in readers' estimates of her worth. Perhaps this ought to make us wary of accepting completely Anne's own final rejection of her individual perceptions, her sensitivity to moral and psychological subtleties, in favor of strict convention. We simply cannot feel that she is justified in denying the value of one of her chief virtues so glibly. "How quick come the reasons for approving what we like" (p. 15), says the narrator of *Persuasion*. And surely Anne, at the end of the novel, would not at all like to accept the idea that her long unhappiness was her own fault, the result of a mistaken conception of duty. It is emotionally much easier and more satisfying for her to deny the individual the right to break a major social law on his own discretion and to conclude that her own suffering was an unavoidable result of the fact that codified social wisdom must sometimes be mistaken in particular instances; the hard price that duty sometimes exacts.[14] Interestingly, Anne's speeches justifying her decision are most unusually full, for Anne, of contradictions and non sequiturs. She indicates that she believes Lady Russell's advice to have been mistaken by asserting that she herself would never give such advice, yet she is also sure that the advice was of the sort that depends entirely on the event for its justification, and she assures Capt. Wentworth that she could never have been persuaded to violate the dictates of duty by marrying Mr. Elliot, "a man indifferent to me" (p. 244), although she had previously acknowledged that she might easily have been persuaded to marry him. And in this assertion, further, she strangely ignores the fact it is a woman's duty not to marry a man to whom she is indifferent—but hardly her moral responsibility to make absolutely certain that *he* loves her. Also, *Persuasion* is full of evidence that Mr. Elliot, however great his moral failings may be in general, is sincerely attracted to Anne. This uncharacteristically irrational justification of her previous conduct seems to indicate that Anne, at the end of the novel, is shaping her past into a completely palatable form, so that she will not have to modify the world view to which she is so deeply committed in accordance with its lessons. For we must remember that Anne is a conventional Elliot with a sensitive conscience and has invested an immense amount of suffering in her commitment to propriety—and for all these reasons we cannot quite feel that her final judgment of the issues is not emotionally biased.

Another aspect of propriety which is relevant to Anne's experiences in *Persuasion* relates to handling difficult social situations in accordance with the roles dictated by the major rules. Like Elinor Dashwood, Anne has attempted to deal with the anguish resulting from her broken romance in this way. As the rules suggest, Anne has concealed her disappointment and suffering under a conventional facade of calmness and reserve. When Elinor, in *Sense and Sensibility,* concealed her suffering by playing such a role, she discovered that her pretensions to calmness and control gradually became a reality. In only a few months time, Elinor was able to contemplate her lost love "with little emotion" (p. 263). The role suggested by the major rules of propriety turned out to have had truly healing effects on Elinor's deeply wounded heart. But Anne has been playing Elinor's decorous role for eight whole years and it has not done a thing for her. Beneath her calm and proper facade, Anne's heart is as sore as it was when she first broke her engagement. The only way that the role she has been playing has helped Anne is, as we noted above, by concealing her pain from others. In *Sense and Sensibility,* Jane Austen suggests that obeying the major rules of propriety can be really effective in helping people recover even from severe romantic disappointments. In *Persuasion,* however, though Anne plays the role, "her attachment and regrets had . . . clouded every enjoyment of youth" (p. 28), and Jane Austen concludes that the rules of propriety did little to help. Now, a "second attachment" is "the only . . . sufficient cure" (p. 28) which Jane Austen imagines for Anne. It's hard to say exactly how much of this difference between *Sense and Sensibility* and *Persuasion* is due to the fact that Jane Austen was tackling a different problem in each novel. What I want to note here is simply that, in *Persuasion,* Jane Austen no longer portrays the wisdom of society as particularly effective in protecting the individual from the worst emotional consequences of serious errors of judgment. Following the major rules gets Anne into serious emotional trouble in the first place and continuing to follow them doesn't do much to extricate her. Yet Anne does not give up her commitment to those major rules, in spite of the fact that they have almost invariably been stumbling blocks, rather than supports, for her.

The end of the novel, therefore, leaves us with the problem unresolved. Just as those natural aristocrats of good feeling, the Crofts and Harvilles, are justified in setting their own standards of propriety in minor matters, so, one feels, ought Anne, *Persuasion*'s closest approach to a natural aristocrat of judgment, to be justified in breaking even the major rules of propriety. But Anne is unable to accept the responsibility of free judgment (just as she was previously unable to express her good feeling freely in her manners), and she relies upon the more comfortable assumption that is right to obey the major rules of society and that if obeying those rules results in eight years of unmerited suffering, one will at least be spared the keener pain of self-reproach, of feeling that one has only oneself to blame.[15] Anne probably realizes that if there are to be rules laid down for the general good, then all should obey them, for who is to judge, before the fact, whether he himself is indeed the superior intellect who can judge better than the major rules can direct him? Wentworth's assumption that he had such an intellect was certainly unjustified. If we see Anne's decision in favor of convention purely as the result of a perception that without a set of sacrosanct rules society would be chaos, perhaps we can accept it. But Anne's commitment to the conventions by which she has lived and from which she has suffered has an emotional force of which she is unaware, and this gives rise to a doubt that her affirmation of the major rules is totally rational in nature, particularly since Anne herself formulates no very clear intellectual reasons for this affirmation. At the end of *Persuasion,* Anne states her approval of her own strong need for convention—a trait which, however generally estimable, is not what makes Anne Elliot unique—and she does so at the cost of undervaluing, or indeed, ignoring, the sensitivity of judgment which readers of the novel feel is the unique and uniquely valuable element in her character.

And thus *Persuasion* closes. In it Jane Austen has asserted the right of people of good feeling to make their own rules concerning minor points of propriety, yet she has pointed out the dangers of carrying this practice too far and has observed that some people of good feeling are, for various reasons, unable to free themselves from bondage to even the minor rules of decorum. And she has suggested the possibility—almost completely ignored in *Sense and Sensibility*—

that intelligent individuals may sometimes be better able to judge important questions of human conduct for themselves than the major conventional rules of propriety can do for them. Though Jane Austen has caused her intelligent heroine to reject this possibility, it is upon grounds that seem more emotionally suspect than intellectually convincing. *Persuasion* considers seriously an idea which, in its earlier formulations, had only been scorned in Jane Austen's work: the idea that some individuals can intuit human reality for themselves better than can be done by all the accumulated social wisdom of past and present. Jane Austen is not ready to accept this idea enthusiastically, but she says enough in its favor to make Anne's final rejection of it evidence that she does not quite come up to the novel's ideal of judgment, rather than proof that the idea itself ought to be rejected, as it was in *Sense and Sensibility*. We must not let the fact that the narrator never explicitly censures Anne's viewpoint, that Lady Russell and Capt. Wentworth come to agree that Anne was right, and that Anne herself changes little and never consciously realizes that she is changing at all, lead us to the erroneous conclusion that Anne's acceptance of the major laws of propriety should be endorsed without any critical reservation. When Jane Austen told her niece that the heroine of *Persuasion* "is almost too good for me" (*Letters,* Vol. II, p. 487), she may have meant that Anne's conventionally virtuous manners and opinions are not exactly what she herself, when she wrote this novel, approved as the ideal of human conduct; that Anne's belief in the value of strict external propriety is no longer one Jane Austen is willing to endorse without serious reservations. But then again, perhaps all she meant was that, as an ironist, she would always take greater delight in characters more deeply flawed than Anne. Or perhaps, being Jane Austen, she had both ideas in mind—and more as well.

# NOTES

## Chapter 1

1. The most interesting supporters of this viewpoint are Mary Lascelles, *Jane Austen and Her Art* (London: Oxford University Press, 1939), and A. Walton Litz, *Jane Austen: A Study of her Artistic Development* (New York: Oxford University Press, 1965).

2. Marvin Mudrick, *Jane Austen: Irony as Defense and Discovery* (Berkeley and Los Angeles: University of California Press, 1968), p. 1.

3. D. W. Harding maintains that Jane Austen intentionally makes her destructive criticisms in such a manner as to incur "the minimum risk of setting people's backs up." "Regulated Hatred: An Aspect of the Work of Jane Austen," *Jane Austen: A Collection of Critical Essays,* ed. Ian Watt (Englewood, N.J.: Prentice-Hall, 1963), p. 168.

4. References to Jane Austen's works incorporated in the text are taken from: *The Novels of Jane Austen,* ed. R. W. Chapman, 5 vols., 3d ed. (London: Oxford University Press, 1933).

5. As far as possible, I will try to illustrate the points made in this chapter with evidence drawn from *Pride and Prejudice,* not because this novel is better suited for my purpose than any of the others, but merely to give my argument greater coherence.

6. Andrew Wright, *Jane Austen's Novels: A Study in Structure* (Harmondsworth, Middlesex, England: Penguin Books, 1953), p. 46.

7. See, for example Frank O'Connor: *Mansfield Park* is an "absolute failure" because one "searches vainly for a grin on the narrator's face" when "rancorous, censorious" narrative remarks are voiced. On the basis of these narrative remarks, O'Connor concludes that Jane Austen, the author, is trying "to batter our moral sense" into accepting Fanny as a moral ideal. "Jane Austen: The Flight from Fancy," *Discussions of Jane Austen,* ed. William Heath (Boston: D. C. Heath, 1961), p. 70.

8. Laurence Lerner, *The Truthtellers* (New York: Schocken Books, 1967), p. 151.

9. Henry Austen, "Biographical Notice of the Author," *The Novels of Jane Austen,* ed. R. W. Chapman, V, p. 4.

10. Robert Liddell, *The Novels of Jane Austen* (London: Longmans, 1963), p. 30.

11. The view taken by Mudrick, by Frank O'Connor, by Kingsley Amis, "What Became of Jane Austen?", *Discussions of Jane Austen,* ed. Heath, pp. 99–101, by Gilbert Ryle, "Jane Austen and the Moralists," *Critical Essays on Jane Austen,* ed. B. C. Southam (New York: Barnes & Noble, 1968), pp. 106–122, by Tony Tanner, "Jane Austen and the 'Quiet Thing': A Study of *Mansfield Park,"* *Critical Essays on Jane Austen,* ed. Southam, pp. 136–161, by Robert Garis, "Learning Experience and Change," *Critical Essays on Jane Austen,* ed. Southam, pp. 60–82, and many others.

## Chapter 2

1. Generally the terms can be used interchangeably, but decorum tends to have slightly more formal and solemn overtones.

2. By present-day standards, Jane Austen's relatively estimable characters are all quite conventional and proper in their behavior—and this is true even of the more extreme cases, like Marianne Dashwood. The difference between Marianne's impropriety and Elinor's conventionality may seem to us like the difference between Tweedle dum and Tweedle-dee. For Jane Austen, however, the slight and subtle differences between Marianne's standard and Elinor's, or between Captain Wentworth's and Anne's, are important and raise significant questions about the relationship of the individual to society.

3. References to Jane Austen's letters incorporated in the text are taken from: *Letters, 1796–1817* ed. R. W. Chapman, 2 vols. (New York: Oxford University Press, 1955).

## Chapter 3

1. Cf. Ian Watt: Jane Austen assumed the actual "configurations of society" to be "unalterable." To leave society altogether or to change it radically are not viable possibilities for her characters. "On *Sense and*

*Sensibility," Jane Austen: A Collection of Critical Essays,* ed. Watt, p. 50.

2. The role of a mother whose daughter is conducting a dangerous-looking romance is considered in *Sense and Sensibility,* though not in any detail. Mrs. Dashwood's disregard of the conventional parental role, her refusal to interfere in any way when Willoughby's behavior to Marianne begins to seem suspicious, parallels Marianne's disregard of conventional rules and turns out just as badly. But though Mrs. Dashwood later regrets "her own mistaken judgment" (p. 335) in encouraging Marianne's excesses, the point is not given much importance —for Marianne has been considered throughout as a free agent acting upon *her* own judgment, and not much influenced by the advice of others.

3. This is not to say that the rules of propriety do not provide young men with many other ways of expressing their intentions. Of course they do, but for Jane Austen the proposal alone makes it an engagement— other sorts of attentions only constitute a courtship, which may well prove abortive.

4. For a good, short discussion of sensibility as a literary and historical phenomenon, see Watt, "On *Sense and Sensibility," Jane Austen: A Collection of Critical Essays,* ed. Watt, pp. 44–45.

5. Of course, Willoughby leads Marianne on and gives her all the conventional signs that he is courting her. She may quite reasonably and properly expect a proposal from him, but Jane Austen's point is that it is not proper for her to act as if an engagement exists *before* he has proposed.

6. See Robert Liddell's reasoning on this point: Edward "easily could have released himself from an entanglement dating from his minority. Mrs. Ferrars might have been ill-tempered about it, but she would have paid off Lucy." *The Novels of Jane Austen,* p. 29.

7. Cf. W. A. Craik: Jane Austen never directs irony at Elinor "because she has created a character so faultless that ridicule is impossible." *Jane Austen: The Six Novels* (London: Methuen & Co. Ltd, 1965), p. 33. Or Marvin Mudrick; Jane Austen tries to gain the reader's approval for Elinor "by her deliberate, protective exclusion of Elinor from the focus of irony." *Jane Austen: Irony as Defense and Discovery,* p. 74.

8. Marvin Mudrick, *Jane Austen: Irony as Defense and Discovery,* p. 63.

9. This might be seen as a reversed version of the "delayed rhetorical irony" described in chapter one. Here a point of view which the narrator

at first appears to be ridiculing later turns out to have been perfectly correct.

10. Kenneth Moler, *Jane Austen's Art of Allusion* (Lincoln, Nebraska: University of Nebraska Press, 1968), p. 62ff.

11. See *Sense and Sensibility* p. 7, p. 20, p. 48, p. 80, p. 85, p. 156, p. 312, p. 315, p. 334, p. 335, p. 336, p. 338, p. 346, and p. 356 for hints of the favoritism toward Marianne that Mrs. Dashwood displays. The question of whether Elinor's rational and sensible viewpoint on life is, in part, the result of a purely emotional (i.e. irrational) reaction to her mother's preference for Marianne is one of those ironies which Jane Austen does not attempt to define very precisely.

12. Both sisters, as I remarked earlier, see themselves as devotees of reason. Elinor opposes inductive reason to intuitive judgment, and Marianne opposes intuitive reason to an unthinking slavery to convention.

13. The conversations deals solely with "Lady Middleton's engagements and . . . whether Mr. Palmer and Col. Brandon would get farther than Reading that night" (p. 304).

14. One piece of evidence for this assertion is to be found in a conversation between Marianne and Elinor after the latter has told the former the substance of Willoughby's confession. In this conversation, Elinor refers to Willoughby as "selfish." Marianne, though she is aware that Willoughby has seduced and abandoned Eliza Williams and has jilted herself, answers, lips quivering, " 'Selfish?' " in a tone implying "do you really think him selfish?" —as if this is by far the worst accusation that has yet been made against him.

15. There is no honest, manly ambition which expects to be rewarded fairly for services performed (like Capt. Wentworth's in *Persuasion*) in the world of *Sense and Sensibility*.

16. The major rules of propriety at issue here are, as we shall see in chapter eight, somewhat different in their implications from the major rules considered in *Persuasion*—the only other novel in which the validity of major, as opposed to minor or everyday, rules of propriety is seriously questioned.

17. A point which is frequently made in contemporary novels attacking the cult of sensibility.

18. Evidence for this may be found in the consistent tendency of the novel's "sensibility" characters to forget previous attachments more quickly than do the "sense" characters. Marianne's attachment to Norland is transferred to Barton long before Elinor ceases to regret her

old home. And after Willoughby deserts Marianne, Mrs. Dashwood is sure there was always something in his eyes she did not like and that she has actually preferred Col. Brandon almost from the beginning. In *Persuasion,* the same point is made in the character of Capt. Benwick, a devotee of romantic literature who forgets his dead fiancée in record time.

19. As Elinor learns when she condemns her heart for the "lurking flattery" (p. 357) of the irrational belief, which persists in the midst of all her rational attempts to repress her feeling for Edward, that some day they will be able to marry after all.

# Chapter 4

1. Not even Marvin Mudrick criticizes Elizabeth for "forced yielding to social convention" as he does Elinor—and it seems to me that any character who satisfies Mudrick's standards of unconventionality is likely to satisfy most readers in this respect. *Jane Austen: Irony as Defense and Discovery,* p. 62.

2. Elizabeth does indeed end up with a muddy petticoat—but the point is, as she herself realizes, that she is still " 'very fit to see Jane— which is all I want' " (p. 32).

3. Few critics devote much attention to this episode, which I think is an important one. E. M. Halliday does remark that "the violent outward action in *Pride and Prejudice,* perhaps, is Elizabeth's leap over a puddle on her way to Netherfield." "Narrative Perspective in *Pride and Prejudice,*" *Twentieth-Century Interpretations of Pride and Prejudice,* ed. Rubinstein (Englewood, N.J.: Prentice-Hall, Inc., 1969), p. 80. If this episode seems violent, for this very restrained novel, perhaps the reason is that Elizabeth's walk serves as a physical symbol of her conscious violation of a rule of decorum—always a surprising, or even shocking, act in Jane Austen's books.

4. Thus, later in the novel, Elizabeth refuses to question Lydia about Darcy's presence at her marriage to Wickham. Elizabeth is terribly curious about the matter, but will not ask because Lydia, though perfectly willing to tell, has mentioned that Wickham doesn't want her to discuss it.

5. Elizabeth is aware that her father's behavior as a husband violates both "conjugal obligation and decorum" in a "highly reprehensible manner" (p. 236). It is only poetic justice that Mr. Bennet, who manip-

ulates the forms of decorum in a way that completely disregards their purpose, should have daughters like Kitty and Lydia who are unaware that those forms have any purpose at all.

6. Here are a few examples: *Northanger Abbey,* p. 147, *Sense and Sensibility,* p. 281, *Emma,* pp. 324–5, and *Persuasion,* pp. 232–6. In each of these cases a conversation is overheard in a crowded room primarily because the speakers are not aware that a highly interested person is avidly listening. The clearest example is in *Persuasion,* where Captain Wentworth writes, "You sink your voice, but I can distinguish the tones of that voice when they would be lost on others" (p. 237).

7. Some readers think Elizabeth misjudges Wickham's manners because she is sexually attracted to him. As I indicated in chapter one, I think Elizabeth is really attracted to Darcy and is only pretending to herself that she is in love with Wickham. It is interesting that the two men Elizabeth consciously considers marrying in the first half of *Pride and Prejudice*—Wickham and Col. Fitzwilliam—never seriously intend to marry her. If, as I believe, she is avoiding a sexual commitment to the rather threatening Darcy, it is natural that she should distract her own attention from this problem by inventing romances which have no real possibility of working out.

8. This is what Darcy senses when he observes, at the start of their acquaintance, that Elizabeth's "manners were not those of the fashionable world" (p. 23).

9. A. Walton Litz, who believes that Elizabeth "possesses the illusion of total freedom; she looks to nature, rather than society . . . contemptuous of all conventions that restrict the individual's freedom," and other critics who take the same line, are overlooking a shift that occurs in Elizabeth's view of propriety in the first half of the novel. I believe that she begins with a fairly balanced view of the need for conventions and moves toward a more "natural" or unconventional position under the stress of her desire to approve of Wickham and disapprove of Darcy. *Jane Austen: A Study of Her Artistic Development,* pp. 104–5.

10. In this respect Elizabeth showed her father's influence and proved herself a product of the Bennet milieu.

11. Darcy is true to the basic assumption of the novel—that manners mirror character—in his attempt to prove to Elizabeth that his character has changed by showing her that his *manners* are improved.

12. As Lionel Trilling points out when he says that in *Pride and Prejudice* morality is conceived of as personal style. *"Mansfield Park," The Opposing Self: Nine Essays in Criticism* (New York: Viking Press, 1955), pp. 206–30.

## Chapter 5

1. The problem of dating *Northanger Abbey* is ultimately impossible to solve. According to Cassandra Austen's note it was written after *First Impressions* (the original version of *Pride and Prejudice*) and either concurrently with or after the first draft of *Sense and Sensibility*, in 1797 and 1798. The story to which Cassandra Austen refers almost certainly was (or was a draft of) the manuscript *Susan*, which Jane Austen sold to a publisher in 1803. In her advertisement for the novel, written in 1816, Jane Austen states that Northanger Abbey was "finished" in 1803, which implies that it was revised at that time (*NA*, p. 12). In 1809 the book had still not been published and Jane Austen wrote to the publisher offering to supply another copy—on which she may or may not have been working in the interim. After the publication of *Emma*, the Austens bought back the still unpublished manuscript. Jane Austen's advertisement shows that the book was prepared for the press in 1816. How thoroughly Jane Austen revised it at this time, we cannot know, but apparently she remained unsatisfied with her efforts and decided to shelve the book for the present. It did not, in fact, come out until after Jane Austen's death. The available evidence seems to support Robert Liddell's conclusion that *Northanger Abbey* "is therefore a book which had been written during most of her adult life . . . hardly any part of the book can be securely dated." *The Novels of Jane Austen*, pp. 1–2. It seems to me that in *Northanger Abbey*, Jane Austen makes use of ideas about propriety which are very similar to, but much less formally and abstractly worked out than, those she employs in *Pride and Prejudice*. In order that the reader can make use of the distinctions between "basically moral" and "merely fashionable" rules, which I discuss at some length in my chapter on *Pride and Prejudice*, rather than because I am convinced it is in any meaningful sense a later work, I am discussing *Northanger Abbey* after *Pride and Prejudice*.

2. Similar points about the value of didactic fiction are made in *Mansfield Park* and *Persuasion*.

3. Emma Woodhouse shows something of this same tendency in the "literary" fantasies she invents concerning Harriet Smith's illegitimacy and Jane Fairfax's illicit romance with Mr. Dixon.

4. These are some of the traits which are parodied in a still more extreme form in "Love and Freindship," a literary burlesque written when Jane Austen was fifteen.

5. Most of the rules which the general violates in spirit, though he obeys them superficially, are minor rules governing everyday social interactions. But the general treats the major rules which prescribe his role as a father in the same cavalier fashion. Thus the superficial deference toward Eleanor's wishes which General Tilney expresses really only glosses over his most improper parental tyranny towards her.

6. Catherine's earlier gothic illusions, it might be added, are quite different from her mistake about General Tilney's character. Her fantasies about the mysterious cabinet and the antique chest which she finds in her room merely to be the results of an imagination excited not only by gothic fiction, but also by the unfamiliarity of Northanger and (in the case of the cabinet) by the lateness of the hour and the violence of the storm raging outside. Anyone who, after reading a mystery story late at night, has been afraid to put out the light, will have no trouble understanding Catherine's emotional state when she examines the cabinet—or how silly the whole incident appears the next morning. But Catherine's gothic fantasies about General Tilney are not merely the products of an overstimulated imagination. For they are serious, if misguided, attempts on Catherine's part to solve the riddle of the general's character in the light of concepts she has derived from literature.

7. It is also what Isabella and John Thorpe are trying—but with less success than the general—to do. Both Thorpes are attempting to behave exactly as they want, yet without violating the rules of propriety openly enough to get themselves into trouble. But because their egotism and stupidity are so extreme, and their understanding of the rules of propriety so sketchy, their pretensions are very poorly supported.

# Chapter 6

1. Kingsley Amis, for example, concludes that Fanny "is a monster of complacency and pride who, under a cloak of cringing self-abasement, dominates and gives meaning to the novel . . . because Jane Austen's judgment and her moral sense were corrupted" when she wrote it. "What Became of Jane Austen," *Jane Austen: A Collection of Critical Essays,* ed. Watt, p. 144.

2. In *Pride and Prejudice,* for example, there are many such characters —Sir William Lucas, Mr. Collins, Mary Bennet, Mrs. Jenkinson, Maria Lucas, Mrs. Phillips, etc. But in *Mansfield Park* there is only one char-

acter, Lady Bertram, whose dependence upon others is so great and whose involvement with the world around her so slight that she is never really called upon to make a moral decision that will affect either herself or others.

3. There is only one character, Dr. Grant, whose classification seems at all uncertain and this is probably because we see so little of him. And there is only one character, Tom Bertram, who switches categories in the course of the novel. This happens, however, at the very end of the book, offstage.

4. The other young Prices don't look very promising, morally, when Fanny visits them at Portsmouth. However, at the end of the novel we learn of their "general well doing and success . . . all assisting to advance each other" (p. 473). Somewhere along the way, apparently, they have found their feet, developing purpose and generosity—and the reasons why this happens to *all* of them, in spite of their bad background, will become clear later in this chapter.

5. This is why Edmund and Fanny are so hard on Mary Crawford's disrespectful remarks about her uncle. Their disapproval demonstrates more than mere "readiness to be shocked," as Amis believes. "What Became of Jane Austen," *Jane Austen: A Collection of Critical Essays,* ed. Watt, p. 142.

6. In "Letter the first, from a Mother to her Friend," in "A Collection of Letters," one of her juvenilia, Jane Austen also ridicules the idea of a young girl's coming out into a world in which she has really been living all her life. *Minor Works,* pp. 150–52.

7. Therefore I cannot accept Marvin Mudrick's contention that in *Mansfield Park* "the genteel orthodoxy of Jane Austen's time," represented by Sir Thomas, is proved "categorically superior." Whether we define, as I do, the Crawfords' world as the orthodox one, or whether, like Mudrick, we see Sir Thomas as orthodox, we are forced to conclude that orthodoxy has gone astray and needs to be purified. *Jane Austen: Irony as Defense and Discovery,* p. 155.

8. The factors of natural moral equipment, domestic example, and formal education are all considered, in *Mansfield Park,* as possible causes of the moral differences among its characters—and all are rejected. See, for example, the passage in which Jane Austen pokes fun at the idea that the usual gentlewoman's education can have any influence at all on her moral character (pp. 18–19).

9. It is interesting that this is the only light in which the high-status young people in the novel do regard a profession. Henry Crawford assumes that after Edmund takes orders he "will still live at home"

spending his unearned income "all for his menus plaisirs" (p. 266), and Mary sees a profession solely as an evil to be avoided if possible. ("'A man might escape a profession'" with such an estate [p. 161], she remarks of Mr. Rushworth.)

10. Mrs. Norris, Mrs. Price, and Lady Bertram form a pattern of variations on this theme. Mrs. Norris has no legitimate object on which to employ the excessive amount of energy she possesses, for she is first a clergyman's wife and then a widow, with no children and no real duties. Fanny, comparing her mother to Mrs. Norris realizes that the latter would have made a "respectable mother of nine children, on a small income" (p. 390)—for Mrs. Norris's energies are not evil in themselves, but have turned evil by gradual degrees because no good and compelling employment has ever been provided for them. Her sister, Lady Bertram, on the other hand, has very little energy or talent and what she does have finds sufficient employment in the conventional "duty" of her affluent situation, to sit "nicely dressed on a sofa" (p. 19). The third sister, Mrs. Price, completes the pattern. If Mrs. Norris has energies, but no legitimate work upon which to employ them, and if Lady Bertram has just enough energy to fulfil the minimal demands of her situation, then Mrs. Price has a situation—the poor mother of nine—demanding energy and talent, but lacks the energy and talent to fill it well.

11. As A. Walton Litz points out, one of the aspects of *Lovers's Vows* which Jane Austen's contemporaries found objectionable was the "contempt for social form" it displayed. *Jane Austen: A Study of her Artistic Development*, p. 125.

12. To a startling degree, Henry sees the world and his own character as malleable things which he can form into any shape he wants. He sees himself as capable of playing any sort of theatrical role and imagines himself a clergyman and a conscientious country gentleman, as well as a sailor. When he discusses possible improvements upon Edmund's house at Thornton Lacey, Henry suggests a scheme of alterations practically amounting to the total demolition of the property—failing completely to see that it is easier for a rather poor man to try to fit his needs to the house he owns, than it is for him to create, as Henry suggests, an almost totally new dwelling.

13. And further, this is why Fanny's humorlessness is treated with approval—as evidence of moral earnestness and sincerity.

14. I hope that this discussion has made it clear that I differ from Lionel Trilling ("Mansfield Park," *The Opposing Self*) on the subject of theatrical roles. Trilling believes Jane Austen to disapprove of acting

because she fears the fragmenting effects playing a role will have on the integrity of the self. I think she sees the desire to act mainly as a symptom of an already fragmented self—but does not view acting itself as something that will seriously undermine it further.

15. This was also Jane Austen's belief when she treated the question of judgment in *Sense and Sensibility*.

16. My view of the characters in *Mansfield Park* contrasts with Howard Babb's. He holds that Fanny is unlike all the other characters in the novel because she alone "retains that degree of objectivity which allows her to judge herself," while they judge the world only in terms of their own desires. *Jane Austen's Novels: The Fabric of Dialogue.* (Columbus: Ohio State University Press, 1967), p. 150.

17. In this respect, Mrs. Norris resembles John and Isabella Thorpe in *Northanger Abbey*.

18. Robert Liddell agrees with Fanny that Henry Crawford's behavior at Portsmouth is "delicate and beautiful" and demonstrates a reformed character. *The Novels of Jane Austen,* p. 8. I think, however, that Henry's polite maneuvering to get Fanny alone and his carefully worded hints designed to flatter her while escaping Susan's observation show that he is manipulating the proprieties in the same self-interested way at Portsmouth, as he did in his flirtations at Mansfield. The change seems mainly in the way Fanny perceives him.

## Chapter 7

1. Lionel Trilling, *"Emma* and the Legend of Jane Austen," *Jane Austen: Emma: A Selection of Critical Essays,* ed. David Lodge (London: Macmillan & Co., Ltd, 1968), p. 153.

2. Nearly every critic of *Emma* takes a position on this question, ranging from Mudrick, "Emma is, of course, an inveterate snob," *Jane Austen: Irony as Defense and Discovery,* p. 185, to J. F. Burrows, who believes that Emma is not snobbish at all but merely employs the language of snobbery "to express her wrath, whatever its basis." *Jane Austen's Emma* (Sydney: Sydney University Press, 1968), p. 27.

3. Indeed, she forgets its existence so completely that she can unembarrassedly allude to Jane Fairfax's position as a potential governess in Mrs. Weston's presence, completely forgetting that Mrs. Weston has ever been anything to her but " 'my friend and my dearest friend' " (p. 201).

4. Both Mary Lascelles, *Jane Austen and her Art,* pp. 68–70 and Kenneth Moler, *Jane Austen's Art of Allusion,* pp. 155–186, suggests

that Emma's unorthodox ideas about society may in part be derived from her reading.

5. Like Elinor Dashwood's.

6. Like Fanny Price's or Edmund Bertram's.

7. Frank Bradbrook feels that Emma is always aware that Mr. Elton's manners are "mediocre, inelegant," but approves them as "good enough for his station in life." *Jane Austen: Emma* (London: Edward Arnold, Ltd, 1961), p. 21. It's true that Emma never believes Mr. Elton's manners to come up to the high standard she sets for herself, but she also originally overestimates their quality.

8. Burrows, *Jane Austen's Emma*, p. 38.

9. All the critics I have read agree with Mrs. Charles Malden that Mr. Knightley is "from head to foot a gentleman," and that he is the embodiment of the genteel as it is defined in *Emma*. "A Thorough English Gentleman," *Jane Austen: Emma: A Selection of Critical Essays*, ed. Lodge, p. 60. It is interesting to notice, however, that as an embodiment of true gentility, Mr. Knightley is shorter of ready money, works harder at homelier pursuits, shows a less class-oriented sense of values, and is more unorthodox in his social behavior than any of the other gentlemen who approach the ideals of gentility defined in Jane Austen's earlier novels. A comparison with Mr. Darcy after his reformation, in these respects, is striking.

10. Emma's only social sin in the first half of the novel is her failure to call on the Bates family as frequently as she ought—and this sin of omission is an easy one to forget.

11. Burrows, *Jane Austen's Emma*, p. 110.

12. Bradbrook discusses similarities between *Emma* and *The Way of the World*. *Jane Austen: Emma*, p. 15.

13. It is ironic that Emma should somewhat overestimate Mr. Knightley's disdain of "trick" here. Her opinions, like Marianne Dashwood's, do tend to excess and her understanding of Mr. Knightley is not yet perfect.

# Chapter 8

1. However, I had better remark at the outset that Jane Austen herself did not submit the manuscript of *Persuasion* to a publisher—this was done by her family after her death. It is my feeling that Jane Austen would have revised this book extensively has she lived, but I certainly do not have the effrontery to pretend to know exactly how she

would have changed it. Perhaps the real ironic tangle that marks her handling of propriety in *Persuasion* would have been simplified or partially resolved in revision. But, as Marvin Mudrick remarks, "here is the book and as it is we must judge it." This is, perhaps, his only indisputable statement about Jane Austen. *Jane Austen: Irony as Defense and Discovery*, p. 240.

2. In this respect they resemble Emma before her change of heart.

3. As the idea that elegance is a quality worth seeking was rejected in *Emma,* so in *Persuasion* the quality is generally spoken of with contempt, except insofar as it is one of Anne's attributes.

4. I can hardly agree with Mudrick, however, that *Persuasion* contains Jane Austen's "first admission that life . . . may be very dull for the landed gentry." *Jane Austen: Irony as Defense and Discovery*, p. 208. All her novels, in my view, openly acknowledge that dullness and suggest that only individuals of real worth can use their surplus leisure with dignity and good sense. See the earlier discussions of *Sense and Sensibility* and *Mansfield Park*.

5. The passage is over two pages long. Here is a sample: "Mary's declaration was, 'I hate sending the children to the Great House, though their grandmamma is always wanting to see them, for she humors and indulges them to such a degree, and gives them so much trash and sweet things, that they are sure to come back sick and cross for the rest of the day.'—And Mrs. Musgrove took the first opportunity of being alone with Anne, to say, 'Oh! Miss Anne, I cannot help wishing Mrs. Charles had a little of your method with those children . . . in general they are so spoilt! . . . Mrs. Charles knows no more how they should be treated—Bless me, how troublesome they are sometimes—I assure you, Miss Anne, it prevents my wishing to see them at our house so often as I otherwise should. I believe Mrs. Charles is not quite pleased . . .'" etc. (pp. 44–45).

6. In fact, after making the point at length, in the episode discussed above, that the Musgroves' impropriety of feeling is connected with the impropriety of behavior, Jane Austen rarely recurs to this theme and stresses the Musgroves' basic goodheartedness much more heavily throughout the remainder of the novel (presumably the Musgroves, with a serious illness and two engagements in their family, are no longer bored and restless).

7. As W. A. Craik points out: "This is in striking contrast to *Pride and Prejudice* in particular, where social propriety is almost equated with virtue." In *Pride and Prejudice* virtuous individuals may sometimes disobey rules of propriety, but they must do it only on the basis of

sober consideration, never merely through impulse. *Jane Austen: The Six Novels,* p. 181.

8. Perhaps it should be pointed out that hostile "expressions begun and suppressed" in such a situation represent fairly extreme impropriety of behavior for an intelligent character in Jane Austen's novels, where control of social behavior is usually so firm.

9. Thus, Anne's commitment to the proprieties may, in part, be seen as a result of her family's influence on her. Elinor Dashwood's similar commitment to propriety, however, seems a part of her rebellion against the values endorsed by her mother and sister.

10. I cannot, however, agree with those critics who see no change at all in Anne during the action of *Persuasion*. W. A. Craik, for example, believes that Anne "has become wise" long before the story opens. *Jane Austen: The Six Novels,* p. 167.

11. In terms of the impropriety of behavior displayed, this romance resembles that of Marianne and Willoughby.

12. I do not agree with Mudrick that the basic issue here is economic, that Anne refused "to marry Wentworth because he had no money, and because his chances of making his fortune seemed too remote." *Jane Austen: Irony as Defense and Discovery,* p. 230. Mark Schorer also sees economics as the basic reason for Anne's rejection of Wentworth. "Fiction and the 'Matrix of Analogy,'" *Kenyon Review,* 11 (Autumn 1949): 541–560. This view is not entirely mistaken, but it is surely a gross over-simplification of Anne's motives.

13. Of all the characters in the novel, only Anne believes that she would never give her daughter such advice in a situation like hers with Wentworth. This is, of course, the result of her own unhappy experiences. The principle involved here is a major rule of propriety in the sense of a prescribed course of action which is generally considered to be right. It is not, however, the sort of major rule (like that prohibiting correspondence between a man and woman who aren't formally engaged) which is absolutely precise in its meaning and binding in its application. The rule Lady Russell obeys here is a rather vague one and its applicability depends, in part, on an individual estimate of whether the circumstances involved in a particular engagement are really the sort meant by the rule.

14. And this is, as we have seen, pretty much the point made in *Sense and Sensibility* about the sufferings Elinor's commitment to propriety cause her.

15. Again, this is a point which is endorsed, with far less ironic ambiguity, in *Sense and Sensibility*.